motorcar for the multitudes," Ford had said. "It will be large enough for the family but small enough for the individual to run and care for. It will be constructed of the best materials, by the best men to be hired, after the simplest designs that modern engineering can devise. But it will be so low in price that no man making a good salary will be unable to own one."

On all counts, the Model T made good on that promise. It was a sturdy, efficient—and not altogether unattractive—four-cylinder vehicle that sold for $850. According to Ford promotional material, the Model T was a marvel of design and engineering: reliable but not intimidating; in fact, it was often said that anybody with a screwdriver, a monkey wrench, and a pair of pliers could fix the Model T in the event that it broke down.

Not that anyone, least of all Ford, expected it to be a problem. Far from it. The Model T, whose engine generated 20 horsepower, was a tough, resilient, affordable car that was chiefly responsible for putting America on wheels. From the cities to the farms, it became wildly popular and soon earned such endearing nicknames as "flivver" and "Tin Lizzie." The automobile population swelled, from one car for every 1.5 million people in 1902 to one car for every 800 people in 1909. By 1920 two million cars would be sold annually in the United States, and more than half were Fords. By 1927, the final year of production, more than 15 million Model T's had been sold.

Ford committed himself to producing a car for the masses and the rural masses in particular. Ford grew up on a farm and hated farm work as a boy. The Model T was designed to liberate farmers from the tedious and dirty work of taking care of horses. It could go through the mud on mostly dirt roads, climb hills, and even be used to drive farm equipment. The demand for the Model T far outstripped Ford's capacity to produce them.

David Lewis
Automotive historian

"The Model T was dependable and versatile," observes automotive historian David Lewis. "It was reliable. It was the car that would get you there and get you back at a time when many other cars would not. So that was its great selling point. Also, the prices dropped through the years and that was a big advantage to the Model T. In addition, the Model T had some innovations, including steering on the left, which appealed to people and later would be adopted by all other cars."

In its first year of production the Model T was available in four different body types and an assortment of hues. In 1913, though, the color option was reduced to one: black. By that time the Model T was something of a cultural icon, thanks in large part to Ford's implementation of the moving assembly line.

Reportedly, he got the idea after observing workers at a meat packing plant. Mass production, utilizing standardized tools and parts and relatively unskilled workers, had dramatically cut the cost of automobile production. But speed was still a barrier. The Model T was so popular that demand far exceeded Ford's ability to produce them. Innovation, rather than invention, proved to be the answer.

In the spring of 1913 the first moving belt was installed in a Ford plant. Rather than assembling an entire piece of equipment, each worker was now responsible for a single task—tightening a bolt, for example—as the piece floated by. Just as Ford had hoped, assembly line time dropped dra-

America On Wheels

THE FIRST 100 YEARS: 1896-1996

America On Wheels

THE FIRST 100 YEARS: 1896-1996

THE COMPANION
TO THE PBS SPECIAL

BY FRANK COFFEY
and
JOSEPH LAYDEN

GPG
GENERAL
PUBLISHING
GROUP, INC

Los Angeles

Publisher: W. Quay Hays
Editor: Colby Allerton
Art Director: Kurt Wahlner
Projects Manager: Trudihope Schlomowitz
Production Manager: Nadeen Torio
Color and Pre-Press Manager: Bill Castillo
Production Artist: Gaston Moraga
Production Assistants: Tom Archibeque, Phillis Stacy and Alan Peak
Copy Editor: George Garrigues

For Information:
General Publishing Group, Inc.
2701 Ocean Park Boulevard
Santa Monica, CA 90405

Very special thanks to: Leslie Kendall and the exceptional Peterson Museum; Otis Meyer and Road & Track; Sandy Saunders,
photographer Doc Kaminski, and the fine staff at Harrah's National Automobile Museum; Holly Jones at AP/Wide World photos;
Jocelyn Clapp and the Bettmann Archive; Lee Dunbar at Dunbar's premium gallery in Milford, MA; Mark Patrick and the Detroit Public Library;
Barbara Wurf; and all who lent their talents and patience to this unusual and wonderful project.

Library of Congress Cataloging-in-Publication Data

Coffey, Frank.
    America on wheels : the first 100 years / by Frank Coffey
        p. cm.
    "The companion to the PBS special."
    Includes index.
    ISBN 1-881649-80-6
    1. Automobiles—United States—History. 2. Automobile
industry and trade—United States—History. I. Title.
TL23.C595 1996
629.222'0973—dc20   96-17682
                                                     CIP

Printed in the USA by
RR Donnelley & Sons Company
10 9 8 7 6 5 4 3 2 1

General Publishing Group
Los Angeles

Table of Contents

DEDICATION

For Maggie, my driving engine—FC
To my father-in-law, Hank, a Ford man—JL

ACKNOWLEDGMENTS

Many thanks to the folks at New York's WNET/13, particularly producer/writer Stephan Moore, who, with gifted producer/writers Michael Penland and Jan Albert, created the blue print for what became the book America On Wheels. Sincere appreciation also to Bill Grant, Linda Patterson, Pam Rosenstein and the indispensable Valerie Linson. Thanks also to Jeff Smith, Mark Walker and Carol Whitmore at the American Centennial Commission; Vicky Ford, at the National Auto Museum and Professor Tom Lewis of Skidmore College.

Much appreciation as well to filmmaker Shelby Newhouse and young pro Hank Henning for their able photographic research. And many thanks to the talented writer C. Rips Meltzer for his eleventh hour help with captions and photo identification and to Tim Cooper, of Proteus Design, for his sage technical advice.

Thanks to our publisher, Quay Hays, for once again pushing the proper buttons in the proper high places to make this book a reality. We also want to thank the consummate professionals at General Publishing Group who managed to produce this beautiful volume under the most intense of deadline pressures, including Peter Hoffman, the production team of Gaston Moraga, Bill Castillo, Tom Archibeque and Phillis Stacy, and, most especially, Colby Allerton and Kurt Wahlner, the book's editor and designer, respectively, for both their talents as well as extraordinary grace under pressure.

INTRODUCTION

BY DOROTHY AND THOMAS HOOBLER

Only a hundred years have passed since the first automobile chugged out of the Duryea brothers' workshop in Springfield, Massachusetts. Yet in that short span of time the automobile has changed the nation in ways that would have astonished the wildest dreamer in 1896.

Almost at once, the automobile became a symbol of romance, individuality, and power. People remembered their first automobile as a rite of passage. Families stood with their cars to be photographed as a sign that they had "made it." Young people regarded a car as the entry to adulthood. It could take them wherever their hopes and dreams beckoned.

Young lovers soon discovered that the automobile allowed them to escape the family parlor and do their wooing in privacy. Moralists condemned the behavior that went on in the back seats of cars, but millions of Americans fondly associate the first stirrings of young love with an automobile.

Cars also gave women the freedom to travel whenever and wherever they wished. Behind the wheel of an automobile, women were indeed any man's equal, able to make choices that determined their own destinies.

Congress passed the first Federal Road Act in 1916, and ribbons of asphalt and concrete began their inexorable march across the nation. Americans in cars set out in search of new jobs, better lives, or simply adventure. The United States became a nation on wheels.

Different makes of automobiles reflected the self-image of their owners. Long-vanished cars still have the power to inspire a burst of nostalgia: the Model T Ford, the Jordan Playboy, Duesenberg, Packard, the 1957 Chevrolet, the Plymouth Barracuda, the Mustang....The list is endless. For an automobile was more than a piece of machinery; it became part of Americans' most cherished memories.

The popularity of the automobile literally drove the American economy in the 20th century. Automobile manufacture became the nation's largest industry and supported the growth of others. By 1930, automobiles consumed 90 percent of the petroleum, 80 percent of the rubber, 75 percent of the plate glass, and 20 percent of the steel from American factories.

The landscape of America changed as new businesses sprang up to meet the needs of automobile users. Filling stations replaced blacksmith shops. Motor hotels (shortened to "motels") offered travelers a place to sleep on the road. "Drive-in" restaurants and movie theaters became part of the American scene. Billboards blocked the view of the natural landscape, and long stretches of roads became cluttered with stores and businesses.

In the post-World War II era, middle class Americans began the move to newly built suburbs, seeking a refuge from the congestion and pollution that automobiles had caused. The focus of American life shifted as an automobile-based culture grew in suburbia. Two-car families, car pools, station wagons (and today, vans) reflected the needs of this new lifestyle. Shopping malls, with acres of free parking spaces, became the center of a society on wheels.

As the first century of the American automobile draws to a close, it is just as difficult to predict the future as it was in 1896. The American love affair with the automobile shows no sign of abating, though the cost of a new car is ten times greater than in 1960 and the supply of gasoline no longer seems limitless. The next century's automobiles may be powered by electric batteries, pollution-free fuel, or even by electronic devices underneath the roads. But a nation without automobiles seems as unimaginable as today's America was a century ago.

PROLOGUE

On eternity's calendar the automobile is but an infant. The first gasoline-powered vehicle was sold in the United States in 1896, and, like any new baby, it was at once miraculous and maddening. One hundred years later, not much has changed; and yet, everything has changed.

Indeed, no single invention has so dramatically affected life in the 20th century. Ours has become a society totally dependent on the automobile. Remarkably, there are more than 175 million licensed drivers in America, and over 200 million cars. With approximately 2.3 million workers, the automobile industry is easily the largest U.S. employer. And, of course, it feeds a vast network of ancillary businesses, all of which would disappear from the economic landscape if the automobile somehow ceased to exist.

It wasn't so long ago that our lives ran in small circles, constricted by limited personal mobility. The automobile changed all of that. It rendered the horse and buggy obsolete. It expanded our world, permitting migration, exploration, settlement...opportunity, on a grand, unimagined scale. Today there are endless stretches of highway, providing access to vast expanses of heretofore unreachable wilderness as well as every pocket of civilization. We have become a nation on wheels, a people obsessed with moving, with the freedom of mobility, with the pure joy of motoring.

For Americans the automobile is like a magic carpet, fulfilling our every wish, whisking us away to pursue a new world defined only by the reach of our imaginations.

As we reflect on America's passionate, often irrational love affair with the automobile, though, it becomes apparent that the relationship remains tempestuous. If the first belch from the first internal combustion engine was met with a mix of apprehension and euphoria, so too does the car culture of the 1990s provoke a sense of ambivalence. Lord knows, the horseless carriage still has its critics.

Even car lovers acknowledge, if grudgingly, the pollution, the safety issues, the clogged highways that stretch from coast to coast. But, as in any relationshp, they remain in love despite recognizing the loved one's imperfections. It is, at base, quite simple: Americans have a fervent, intense, enduring love affair with their cars.

Detroit's penchant for downsizing and outsourcing notwithstanding, the automobile population boom continues unabated. Each year fifteen million new automobiles roll off the assembly lines, helping American motorists travel nearly two a half trillion miles. More than ever, it seems, we are hopelessly addicted to our cars, and to the romance of the open road— even if it isn't quite as open as it once was. The automobile remains not only our primary mode of transportation, but the central object of American culture, a mechanical beast we cannot hope to tame. It is its very power, its capacity to change our lives, to open up possibilities, that we find so irresistible, and that we celebrate in this centennial.

Frank Coffey, New York, New York
Joseph Layden, Saratoga Springs, New York

Part One

Driving Force

The infamous Vanderbilt Cup Race (1904-1910) was the most popular racing event of its time until safety concerns forced organizers to cancel it. Note how close the crowd stands to the cars, which were already achieving top speeds of well over 100 mph by 1909. Lacking the steering and brakes of today's cars, it's not surprising that far more pedestrians were killed at road races than drivers.

At the finish line, for example, crowds had to be hosed off the track in advance of the speeding cars or else they'd fail to move in time. Whether hosed in time or not, it always made for an exciting finish.

CHAPTER 1

The Horseless Carriage

A s dawn broke on the morning of September 20, 1893, four men pushed a small, four-wheeled buggy out of a barn in Springfield, Massachusetts. One of the men, 23-year-old J. Frank Duryea, climbed aboard the odd-looking contraption and began toying with its steering tiller, preparing for the shortest, but most eventful, journey of his life.

Four years earlier, Frank's older brother, Charles E. Duryea, then a 27-year-old bicycle manufacturer in Peoria, Illinois, had read a story in *Scientific American* detailing the revolutionary work of a German inventor named Karl Benz. According to the article, Benz had succeeded in constructing a self-propelled road vehicle powered by an internal combustion engine. Charles Duryea had been thinking of just such an invention,

The two-cylinder Duryea Motor Wagon may not have been the first self-propelled road vehicle, but it was the first to come off an automobile production line. The Duryea brothers manufactured 13 of them in 1896 and the American automobile industry was born.

and news of Benz's accomplishments moved him to action. He became obsessed with the notion of creating his own version of the horseless carriage, and it wasn't long before Frank Duryea, a machinist, joined Charles in chasing this dream.

A bicycle production contract with the Ames Manufacturing Company brought the brothers to Massachusetts, but in their spare time they worked feverishly on plans for a gasoline-powered engine. Business interests compelled Charles to return to Peoria in late 1892, but Frank remained in Springfield. With the help of a private investor named Erwin Markham, the project survived. Frank redesigned the engine, tinkered with the chassis of a buggy, and formulated a way to make it work. Or so he hoped. In the summer of 1893

he wrote optimistically to his brother: "I have got the carriage almost ready for the road. I will take it off somewhere so that no one will see us have the fun."

"Somewhere" turned out to be a barn on the outskirts of town owned by Howard Bemis, the brother-in-law of Erwin Markham. Also present was Rudy MacPhee, a reporter for the Springfield *Evening Union*. Frank Duryea was no fool. He wanted to test his invention in relative privacy. No crowds. No pressure. At the same time, he wanted to be sure the event was properly chronicled.

Frank Duryea's maiden voyage began with a hand signal. Markham, Bemis, and MacPhee leaned into the buggy and started to push. In less than half a minute, as the carriage picked up speed,

(Opposite page) Charles E. Duryea riding his horseless carriage, which brother Frank used to win the 1895 Chicago Times-Herald "Race of the Century." (Above left) Frank Duryea in his mid-seventies. (Above right) Ransom Eli Olds built the first American steam-powered vehicle in 1887, but rejected steam for gas power. He would become an industry titan rivaling Ford before being taken over by General Motors in 1908.

Racing at Daytona (left) was already a popular annual event by 1905.

(Above and left) Race officials communicate during the 1905 running of the Daytona. Note the bike messenger in the background.

the engine fired. It sputtered, coughed, and rattled to life. Plumes of smoke filled the air as the buggy rolled down Spruce Street, leaving three stunned and exhausted men in its wake.

The trip was brief. Just 200 feet from the starting point, Duryea's vehicle came to a stop when it was unable to clear a six-inch mound of earth. Obviously this was not a carriage suitable for travel. Not yet. Nevertheless, there was cause for celebration. A barrier had been shattered. There would be no turning back.

Whether J. Frank Duryea's buggy was the first in the United States to be powered by a gasoline engine remains a matter of considerable debate. Certainly it was not the first self-propelled road vehicle in the country; throughout the land similarly bright, adventurous young inventors—men who knew that neither the bicycle nor the horse and carriage would be sufficient modes of transportation in the 20th century—were pushing the envelope of design and technology. In time, recognition and credit would be sought by, among others, Elwood Haynes of Kokomo, Indiana, who in 1894 claimed his was the first "real" car (the Duryeas, he sneered, had merely attached a buggy to an engine); Alexander Winton, the first person to produce and sell an automobile; George Selden, who sought a patent for his design for a gasoline-propelled vehicle as early as 1879; Ransom Eli Olds, a future industry titan who built his first steam-propelled vehicle in 1887; and William Morrison, whose electric automobile was produced in 1891 in Des Moines, Iowa.

"If you were to ask me who invented the automobile, I would have to say everybody," notes automotive historian Richard Scharchburg. "Because the automobile was a device that is so complicated that it required years of evolution in order for it to come to a point where it could be manufactured."

That so many brilliant minds were focused on one idea supports the argument that, by the turn of the century, the United States was thoroughly prepared to embrace the automobile; it was an invention whose time had come. And, for reasons of safety and power, it was generally acknowl-

edged that gasoline was the most logical and effective source of fuel. Today, of course, clogged highways and smog-enshrouded cityscapes prompt a certain degree of cynicism about the automobile and the culture it has fostered, along with dewy-eyed romanticism among those who long for simpler times.

It's only fair to point out, however, that many of the criticisms now leveled at the automobile were once directed at the horse and carriage. Most of the urban problems typically associated with the automobile in the 1990s were common to the horse and carriage in the 1890s: traffic jams, parking problems, noise, accidents, pollution. Of these, the most distressing was the last. While the horse emitted no exhaust, it did emit. A typical horse produced more than 30 pounds of dung each day. One need not be a mathematician to understand that in a city such as New York, with a horse population of approximately 175,000, this amounted to a mountain of manure.

Beleaguered sanitation workers had no hope of keeping pace. Each day streets were shoveled, barges filled, and thousands of pounds of waste flushed into oceans and rivers. Always, though, it was a losing battle. As cities grew, so too did the equine population. In the rainy season of spring the problem was most severe. Piles of frozen manure thawed and mixed with mud, turning roads and streets into steaming, fetid swamps. It was, of course, a rich spawning ground for flies, which bred madly, thus heightening the threat of disease; the horses themselves carried tetanus. Summertime provided little relief. A haze of street dust, comprised primarily of dry horse manure, hung in the air, making it nearly impossible to breathe without difficulty. Respiratory and intestinal infections were prevalent in the summer months, particularly among children who spent too much time outside, inhaling foul air.

Compounding the problem was the tendency of the poor beasts to drop dead on the job. Overworked and often poorly cared for, the urban mare usually met her end in a most ignominious way. After collapsing on the street, she would be

Overworked and poorly cared for, horses frequently collapsed in the street. Fifteen thousand horse carcasses were left to rot on the streets of New York annually. (Right) A typical city street (circa 1900) featuring uncollected garbage, unshoveled manure, and rampant disease. The advent of the automobile age actually improved health conditions, making the horse obsolete and removal of garbage efficient.

unbridled and left to die. By 1890, approximately 15,000 dead horses were removed annually from the streets of New York. Unfortunately, cleanup was far from efficient, and it was common for the carcass to spend several days rotting in the sun before it was finally dragged away. Not only did this contribute to an already unhealthy environment, it also exacerbated a nightmarish traffic situation: too many carriages, narrow streets, and few rules governing the conduct of drivers.

Add to this mess the clattering of hooves on cobblestone streets and the incessant groan of rickety iron wheels—noise pollution so severe that it made ordinary conversation virtually impossible—and the horse-and-carriage era suddenly loses much of its allure. Indeed, the automobile was generally considered a prayer answered at the turn of the century. Not only would it be cleaner than the horse, it would be safer, quieter, more efficient, and cheaper.

An early advocate of the horseless carriage (the term "automobile" would not be popularized until after the turn of the century) was a man named Herman H. Kohlsaat, publisher of the Chicago *Times-Herald*. Kohlsaat was intrigued by an 1894 road race from Paris to Rouen, which was sponsored by the French publication *Le Petit Journal*. It seemed to Kohlsaat that his newspaper could benefit from the publicity associated with such an event, and so he decided to promote a similar contest.

The "Race of the Century," as it came to be called, was held on Thanksgiving Day, 1895. Rules were simple but specific: at least three wheels and two passengers (one driver, one umpire) per vehicle; any fuel other than "muscle power" was acceptable. The 54-mile course would take the contestants from Jackson Park in Chicago to Evanston and back again.

Kohlsaat's hope was that the race would not only help him sell newspapers, but also demonstrate to the masses that the "motocycle" was clearly superior to the horse and carriage. It didn't exactly turn out that way, however. More than a foot of snow fell on Chicago on November 27, one day before the race, making the course nearly impassable in spots. Still, six cars (none with brakes) approached the starting line shortly before 9 a.m. The field included three gasoline-powered Benz models, two battery-powered electric vehicles, and the two-cylinder Duryea Motor Wagon.

The foul weather took its toll on all of the participants that day; in fact, four did not even complete the race. In the end, Frank Duryea emerged the winner. His actual on-road time: 7 hours, 53 minutes. Including time lost to repairs and other stoppages, the total was 10 hours, 23 minutes. His average speed was only five miles per hour. Considering the conditions, it was a remarkable accomplishment, although some newspapers of the day failed to recognize it as such. Critics, for example, were quick to dwell on the fact that only one-third of the field had finished the race. Most observers, though, were duly impressed.

In addition to the $2,000 they received in prize money, the Duryea brothers also became celebrities. The sudden rush of fame allowed them to form the Duryea Motor Wagon Company, and orders began arriving soon after. In February of 1896, the automobile production line (and, unofficially, the American automobile industry) was born, as the Duryea brothers manufactured the first of 13 vehicles. By the end of the year, one

> One of my earliest memories was seeing these two very fancy rich ladies getting into their electric car with their long dresses and their big hats. It was really amazing to us. We all stood there and stared at them because nobody we knew could afford a car.
>
> *Studs Terkel*
> *Writer*

would even be sold to the Barnum & Bailey Circus. It was an odd but notable tribute: When the circus paraded through town, the Duryea Motor Wagon followed the elephants and preceded the horse-drawn cages holding the other animals.

As it happened, 1896 was the best of years for Frank and Charles Duryea. By the end of the century they had split up, their place in history secure, but their partnership—and friendship—destroyed by envy and greed. In the future they would play minor roles in the development of the automobile. The stage, however, had been neatly set for a new cast of characters.

By 1900 at least 100 different brands of horseless carriages were being marketed in the United States. Because they were all virtually handmade, the cars were outrageously expensive. In fact, the masses viewed the early automobile as little more than a high-priced toy for the wealthy, and as such it engendered a great deal of resentment and anger. In the cities and in the countryside, motorists were not greeted kindly.

"The car was a rich man's toy, and to many it was a despicable symbol of arrogance and power," observes automotive historian Ron Edsforth. "There was a growing gap between those on the bottom of society and those on top. America was just emerging from the economic depression of the 1890s.

There was a growing unrest among rural farmers and among the immigrant workforce. It's not surprising that some took to stoning rich people in cars—they scared horses, turned over vegetable carts, hit people, and were a general disruption."

Nevertheless, the horseless carriage was finding its niche, and demand was growing. The United States Army purchased its first automobile around the turn of the century; so did the U.S. Post Office. In major metropolitan areas such as New York, Boston, and Philadelphia, electric cabs, delivery trucks, and ambulances became familiar sights. But it was a blacksmith's son from Lansing, Michigan, who put the automobile on the main streets of America.

Ransom Olds was only 18 when he hooked up a steam engine to a three-wheeled vehicle and took off for a ride around his neighborhood. Olds was a sharp young man, though. He knew that steam engines, while powerful, also required frequent maintenance. And they were dangerous, for they had a tendency to explode. Olds came to the conclusion early that gasoline, which was then abundant and cheap, would fuel the automobile of the future, and so he

An older Ransom Olds poses aboard his celebrated 1901 Oldsmobile Runabout. This early best-seller was the first car manufactured in volume off a production line.

Early Oldsmobiles: Roy D. Chapin posing on his 1902 Olds Runabout, which he drove from New York City to Detroit in just nine days, the first record of this feat (left).

An Olds Runabout with a retractable roof gave this couple confidence to wear their Sunday best (below).

A pair of properly attired drivers take an Olds Runabout with an attachable trunk out for a spin around town (circa 1902) (top right).

A vintage Olds Runabout, carefully restored to its former splendor, still looks ready to be cranked and sputtered about town. Note the extra-thick tires added on at a later date (bottom right).

began work on an internal combustion engine of his own. He also was among the first of the American inventors to recognize the need for an automobile that was merely functional and reliable—a car for the masses.

That vehicle, dubbed the "Runabout," was one of the first produced by the fledgling Olds Motor Works, which—with the help of a private investor named Samuel L. Smith— broke ground in Detroit in late 1899. Over the course of the next year, Olds produced eleven different models varying widely in price and design. He had not yet decided which model would receive the bulk of his company's resources, but on March 9, 1901, fate stepped in and rendered the decision for him. On that day the Olds Motor Works was destroyed by fire. The only vehicle rescued was the prototype for the Runabout—a small buggy with lightweight wheels and a curved dashboard. Powered by a one-cylinder engine similar to those on today's lawn-mowers, the Runabout could handle speeds of three to 20 miles per hour.

For country folks the automobile provided relief from isolation. A woman from Muncie, Indiana, was once asked by a Department of Agriculture interviewer, "Why do you own a Model-T but you don't own a bathtub?" The woman was a little surprised by the question and answered, "You can't go to town in a bathtub."

The automobile just opened up the whole panoply of advantages that were not possible before.

Richard Scharchburg
Automotive historian

Olds viewed the accident not as a disaster, but as a "miracle"—a sign that this was the car that would make his fortune. "My horseless carriage is no passing fad," he claimed in an early advertisement. "It never kicks, never bites, never tires on long runs, never sweats in hot weather, and doesn't require care when it's not in use. It eats only when it's on the road. And no road is too rough or too bad for our Oldsmobile Runabout."

In the case of the Runabout, necessity was

indeed the mother of invention. In order to survive, the financially strapped Olds Motor Works had to engage in volume production before the summer of 1901, when it was presumed that fair weather would bring out a legion of new buyers. So, Olds made a decision that would change the face of automobile manufacturing forever: He contracted with other companies to make some of the parts for his cars. The final product would then be assembled in his factory. With this method, each individual part would be interchangeable—exactly the same as all other parts of the same type. Cars would no longer be made up of hand-made parts that would fit only that particular car. As a result, Olds' assembly line was able to produce a great number of cars in a relatively short period of time.

Several of the subcontractors hired by Olds later became famous for their own accomplishments. For example, transmissions were supplied by the Dodge brothers, John and Horace; engines came from Henry Leland, an exceptionally skilled machinist who would later found Cadillac and Lincoln; bodies were supplied by Fred J. Fisher, whose family went on to become body makers for General Motors.

For now, though, the spotlight was on Ransom Olds, which he did not mind in the least. Olds was a promoter as well as an inventor, and he went about the business of selling his cars with great gusto. First, he adapted the French term *automobile* to meet his own needs and came up with a new name for his car: the Oldsmobile. Then, by pricing the vehicle at a comparatively reasonable $650, he

addressed his target audience: the owner of the horse and buggy.

"Mobility was probably at the heart" of the automobile's popularity, says Richard Scharchburg. "It was so darned attractive that they had this personal mobility at their command. Ransom Olds is kind of a cute example of that. He talked about the advantages of the automobile over the horse. The car was more convenient. It was less expensive. A good team of horses was pretty expensive, you know. And then you had to have the stable. You had to pay for the feed whether the horse was being used or not. And the horse would tire out. I mean, you couldn't go all day with a horse. You eventually could in the automobile. And it was that durability that the automobile was attracting."

To publicize the durability and reliability of the Oldsmobile, Olds sent his assistant, Roy Chapin, on a nine-day, 800-mile trip from Detroit to New York in the fall of 1901. For driver and owner alike, it was quite a gamble. Roads of the time were little more than dirt paths that turned to soup with the slightest rain. Gasoline stations had not yet been invented. And if the car broke down, there were no garages to help with repairs. Chapin was on his own. If he failed, he might be stuck on a lonely road for some time; and Ransom Eli Olds, by extension, would look like a fool.

But he did not fail. On November 6, a mud-splattered Roy Chapin arrived at New York's Waldorf-Astoria hotel, having successfully completed the longest trip by an American automobile. Predictably, newspaper accounts of the journey helped boost interest in the Runabout. Olds sold 425 the first year and 2,500 the next. Production hit a peak in 1904, when the Olds Motor Works sold more than 5,000 Oldsmobile Runabouts. The car's immense popularity was even immortalized in song: "*Come away with me, Lucille, in my merry Oldsmobile. Down the road of life we'll fly, auto-mo-bubbling, you and I.*" Thanks in large part to Ransom Eli Olds, America's love affair with the automobile was blooming.

Barney Oldfield, the dean of American racing drivers, is shown here in 1910 speeding his Blitzen-Benz over the packed sands of Daytona beach at 131.75 mph.

1901

Breer—Engine Type: 2-cylinder, stream. Horsepower: 5. Place Manufactured: Los Angeles. Carl Breer made the steam engine and boiler, the crankshaft and connecting rods, the levers and other controls, and the wooden body. He bought the chassis and gauges and hired local carriage workers to paint the car and upholster the seats. The car has two gears—forward and reverse. Breer restored this car in his later years when he worked at Chrysler in Detroit. Collection of the Natural History Museum of Los Angeles County. (Below) Another early independent: 1900 Packard Model B Runabout.

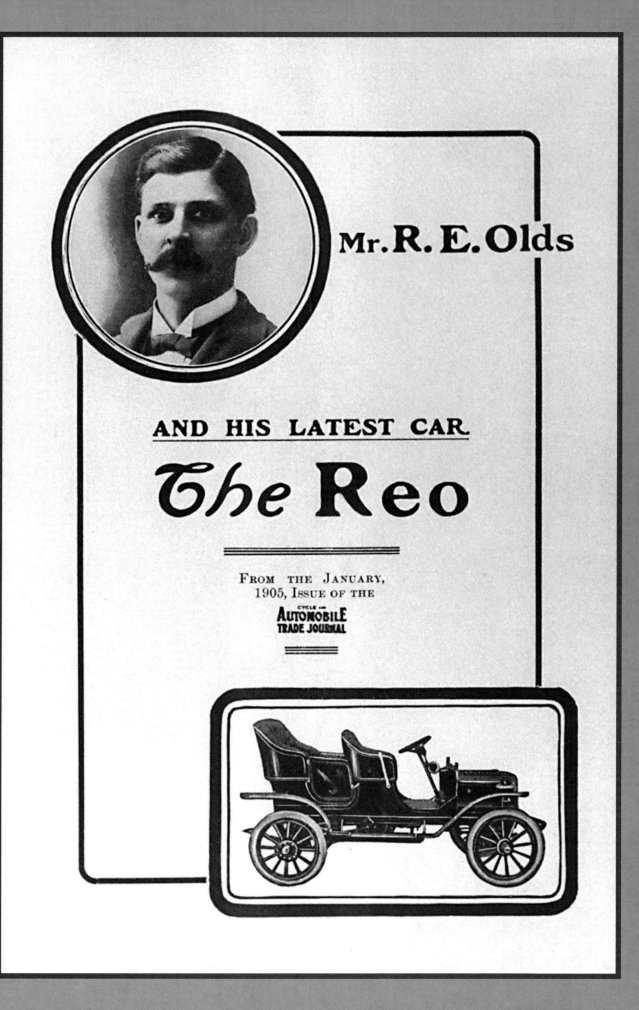

Mr. R. E. Olds

AND HIS LATEST CAR

The Reo

From the January, 1905, Issue of the

Cycle and Automobile Trade Journal

"Charles Duryea had the idea of a car for the masses. So did Ransom Olds," observes Richard Scharchburg. "We had spaces to cover where [railroad] tracks couldn't go. And the advantages of transportation that was within the control of the individual seeking the transport was something that appealed to Americans. They took to the automobile like a duck to water."

Most of them, anyway. Despite the acclaim, the automobile still had not won universal acceptance. Farmers whose horses were frightened by the carriages remained hostile. (In fact, one early rule of the road—seldom enforced—dictated that when an automobile met a horse-drawn carriage, the driver turn off the engine, disassemble the car, and wait by the side of the road until the horse and buggy passed.) Car owners were often the object of ridicule; occasionally they were the target of gunfire. One physician of the time even believed that cars presented a serious health hazard to women. "A speed of 15 to 20 miles an hour in a motor car causes them acute mental suffering, nervous excitement and circulatory disturbances," the doctor wrote.

But there was no halting progress. For better or worse, the automobile was capturing the public's attention. And, thanks in part to a series of promotional activities, the most effective of which was racing, the image was generally appealing. Far from the blue-collar sport it would later become, auto racing in the first decade of the 20th century was a game for society's elite. Millionaire William K. Vanderbilt, one of the great early racers, stored more than 100 cars in his private garage and hired a team of 20 mechanics to keep them running smoothly.

Then, as now, auto racing represented a combination of athleticism, daring, and sexuality. Americans in general, even those who felt the automobile was a menace, were fascinated by its power and speed. How else to explain the massive crowds that turned out to watch the Vanderbilt Cup races on Long Island between 1904 and 1910? As many as 250,000 people would line the course, standing at arm's length from cars whizzing by at speeds in excess of 100 mph. There were few fences or grandstands then, and no concrete walls to protect spectators from marginally skilled drivers and their unpredictable machines.

It was a dangerous game. But then, that was the point, wasn't it? Racing served to further romanticize the automobile. It was a toy and a tool, an instrument whose potential had barely been tapped.

Meanwhile, the pioneers of the industry were looking toward the future. In 1902 Henry Leland walked into Ransom Olds' office and announced that he and his engineers had developed a vastly improved motor, one that would give the Oldsmobile greater power and speed. Best of all, Leland declared, the new motor would cost less to produce than the older one. Much to his dismay, the idea was rejected. Adapting the Runabout to Leland's new engine, Olds claimed, would take too much time. Orders would be delayed, perhaps lost. That, at least, was the official explanation. It's also possible that Olds simply did not want to tamper with success. At the time, his was the most profitable automobile in the country. And Olds was an undeniably autocratic manager—in fact, the company's board of directors

> The automobile gave us mobility, it took us away from our families, it gave us the possibility of moving out of town, across state lines into other countries, other parts of the world, meeting other people, marrying other people. I mean, it opened up the world of possibility. It took us out of our straitjacket.
>
> *Laurel Cutler*
> *Chrysler's first*
> *woman executive*

The large motor car tours before World War I promoted the ruggedness and reliability of this new technology. However, early cars required constant maintenance, as well as the frustrating procedure of literally cranking them to get started, which not infrequently resulted in injuries . . . some as severe as a broken jaw.

MAN WANTED

became so frustrated by his methods that it voted him out in 1904. Ransom Olds later went on to form the Reo Motor Car Company.

As for Henry Leland, he decided to take his idea elsewhere. He struck a deal with the sagging Detroit Automobile Company, which was in the process of liquidating its assets. Using Leland's designs, the company manufactured several prototypes, and the car quickly became a success. Leland's new automobile was the Cadillac, named after the French explorer who had built a fort on the site of what later became the city of Detroit. The Cadillac made its debut at the New York Automobile Show in 1903 and received excellent reviews. It was a strong and stylish little car that reflected its maker's commitment to first-class production and design.

Leland, 60 years old at the time, was a supremely confident and capable man. Throughout his life he had been guided by a principle of excellence. He despised nothing so much as mediocrity. During the Civil War he had produced fine, handcrafted rifles whose parts were manufactured to tolerances of $1/1000$ of an inch; 40 years later he was no less committed to quality. Alfred P. Sloan, who would rise to become president of General Motors in the 1920s, wrote of an early meeting with Leland. Sloan was supplying bearings for Cadillac at the time, and Leland was unhappy with their lack of uniformity. "Mr. Sloan," Leland said icily. "Cadillacs are made to run, not just to sell."

To demonstrate how well the early Cadillac ran, Leland once assigned a member of his engineering staff to drive up the steps of the Wayne County Courthouse in downtown Detroit. If the car could endure such an assault, he reasoned, surely it was a match for any road. The stunt apparently worked, for while the Cadillac was not supposed to be a car for the masses—it was large and expensive and beyond the reach of the typical American consumer—by 1908 it had become one of the best-selling automobiles in the United States.

The industry leader, however, was Buick.

Founded by a former bathtub manufacturer, the company did not begin to turn a profit until long after David Buick himself had been eased out of power. Buick went through several reorganizations before selling its first car in 1904. A few months later William C. Durant took control of the company, and almost immediately it became a formidable player in the automotive game.

Durant was not a mechanical genius. He did, however, have a flair for promotion. And he was willing to take risks. In the early 1880s Durant, then a traveling insurance salesman, was introduced to a man who had received a patent for a new type of horse-drawn cart. Durant bought the patent for $50; a decade later he was a millionaire, with 14 factories churning out more than 150,000 Durant-Dort wagons each year.

In Buick, Durant saw a company with some serious financial problems, but a promising company nonetheless. In short order Durant raised $1.5 million to refinance the operation (reportedly, he sold a half million dollars worth of stock in a single day). Durant exploited his contacts in the carriage business and soon established a distribution network that by 1908 had allowed the Buick Motor Company—headquartered in Flint, Michigan—to sell more cars than any other automaker in U.S. history.

Unfortunately, the man who lent his name to the company tasted little of its success. After working behind the scenes for several years, David Buick left the Buick Motor Company in 1908. By the time he died in 1929, virtually penniless, his namesake motor company had sold more than two million automobiles.

William Durant, meanwhile, became one of the giants of the industry, a larger-than-life figure who thrived on competition. Business, to Durant, was fun. He was a gambler, and so 1908 was undoubtedly one of the greatest years of his life. In a span of just a few short months Durant would watch Ford—on the strength of the revolutionary Model T—supplant Buick as the industry leader, and then would respond with a bold and dramatic move of his own: the formation of General Motors.

The battle had officially been joined.

YOU AUTO BE WITH ME

WHILE THE SPARKER CEASES TO SPARK.-

CHAPTER 2

A Car For the Multitudes

From the day he first saw a steam-powered farm vehicle, Henry Ford never wavered in his determination to build an automobile. That goal was achieved on June 4, 1896, when the Ford "Quadricycle" was introduced. Ford, the son of a Dearborn farmer, was chief engineer for the Detroit Edison Illuminating Company, but his spare time was devoted to working on a horseless carriage in a shed behind his house. When the project was finally completed, Ford realized his quadricycle would not fit through the building's narrow opening, so he used an axe to tear apart one wall. A few minutes later the quadricycle was on its way.

Ford's buggy broke no new ground in the automotive industry—it was merely functional—but it did help boost the reputation and confidence of its 32-year-old creator, who

It didn't take long for a "car culture" to emerge: This postcard, circa 1910, capitalizes on the gay sense of freedom the automobile gave birth to in America.

JOY RIDING AT SENECA, S. D.

became obsessed with the idea of starting his own automobile business. Ford later went to work for the Detroit Automobile Company, but left in anger when his superiors became displeased with his preoccupation with auto racing. He took a certain narcissistic pleasure in getting behind the wheel of his own vehicles, but also believed—and would continue to believe—that the publicity generated by victory on the racetrack was a benefit to the company as well. Ford's experience with the Detroit Automobile Company was so frustrating that he vowed never again to work for another man. From that moment on, Henry Ford would be his own boss. In his own fiercely individualistic manner, he would construct an empire that would radically alter the quality of life in the United States.

"Certainly Henry Ford made a tremendous impact," notes author Studs Terkel. "He is one of the most important figures of the 20th century. I'm talking now about his inventiveness, not about his philosophy."

Indeed, Ford's narrow views on labor-management relations, politics, and race would eventually come under fire, but there is no question that he was a brilliant and ambitious man whose work had a profound effect on American culture. Success, however, did not occur overnight. It wasn't until 1902 that Ford secured sufficient financial backing to start the Ford Motor Company. Among his investors were the Dodge brothers and a Detroit coal dealer named Alexander Malcomson.

Ford's first automobile, the two-cylinder Model A, debuted in 1904 at a cost of $850—a significant amount of money, but not so much that the average citizen could not consider buying one. Like Ransom Olds, Ford understood the secret to surviving in the automobile industry: mass production. Cars, he believed, should look the same and smell the same. They should all perform well, and they should be priced competitively. In that way the broadest possible market could be reached. As Ford would later say, "I'm going to democratize the automobile. When I'm

HENRY FORD COMPANY.

BUILDERS OF
HIGH-GRADE

AUTOMOBILES
AND
TOURIST CARS.

MAKERS OF

AUTOMOBILE
SPECIALTIES
AND
SPARK COILS.

OFFICE AND FACTORY.
1343 CASS AVE.

My Dear Brother

DETROIT, MICH. *January 6th 1902*

If I can bring Mr Fournier in line there is a barrel of money in this business it was his proposition and I dont see why he wont fall in line if he dont I will chalenge him untill I am black in the face. as for managing my end of the racing business I would rather have you than any one else that I know of. My company will kick about me following racing but they will get the advertising and I expect to make $ where I cant make ¢ at manufacturing. we are writing to Mr Fournier

Henry

I will write you again soon

(Counterclockwise from top left) The ambitious Henry Ford, dressed in his 1896 Sunday finest, shows off his new invention, the "quadricycle."

Ford was five years away from getting the funding to start his first company. A decade later, Ford motor cars would outsell all others.

Henry Ford's 1902 letter to his brother emphasizes the "barrel of money" that could be made in the business of selling automobiles if he could only get the financial backing. He wasn't kidding—by 1920 he was a multi-millionaire.

On a freezing day in Detroit, Henry Ford stands proudly beside racing driver Barney Oldfield, who drove the bodiless Ford 999 to a world land speed record of 91.37 mph—in 1904! Without clutch, gears, or seatbelt, Oldfield bravely tillered the beastly 999 into the record books on a frozen lake.

through, everyone will be able to afford one, and just about everyone will have one. The automobile will be taken for granted."

Even a man as confident and intelligent as Henry Ford could not have known how prescient a declaration that was. By 1906 the Ford Motor Company had become the industry leader, a position it maintained for the next 21 years. When one of his partners pushed for production of more expensive models to complement the Model A and the four-cylinder Model N, Ford balked. Eventually this led to Ford's buying out his partner and acquiring majority control of the company.

Ford was held in high regard by the average consumer, in part because of a protracted battle with George Selden, who was finally awarded a patent for his gasoline-powered road engine in 1895—even though he had never actually manufactured a prototype. Selden later sold his patent to the Electric Vehicle Company for $10,000 and a share of royalties. To stave off the threat of lawsuits, the Association of Licensed Automobile Manufacturers was organized. According to terms

of the deal, the A.L.A.M. was assigned the patent and would receive two-fifths of all royalties. The Electric Vehicle Company would also receive two-fifths, and George Selden one-fifth.

If this arrangement was satisfactory to most automobile manufacturers, it was not acceptable to Henry Ford, who stubbornly went about his business. The A.L.A.M. eventually sued the Ford Motor Company for patent infringement. In the eyes of the public, Ford was the little man bravely waging war against a monopoly. If this was a simplification of the case, it nevertheless made for good newspaper copy, and it certainly helped boost sales of Ford automobiles. In 1909 Ford lost in the courts; two years later, however, the decision was reversed on appeal. The Selden patent was found to be valid only when applied to vehicles using specific types of engines, most of which were then hopelessly outdated.

Henry Ford was already riding high by the time of his legal victory. Three years earlier, in 1908, the first of his famed Model T automobiles had rolled off the production line. "I will build a

Henry Ford finally achieved his goal of a "universal car" with the 1908 Model T. Inexpensive and dependable, "Lizzie" quickly outsold all other American cars combined. The Model T was so far ahead of its time, it continued to sell 15,500,000 cars in 19 years.

matically. The experiment began in Ford's magneto department, but was soon implemented throughout the entire Highland Park plant. Constant motion became the hallmark of the Ford Motor Company, and daily production naturally skyrocketed. More than 300,000 cars rolled off the Ford assembly line in 1914; the following year the figure was close to half a million. In time, of course, the moving assembly line would be adopted by every automobile manufacturer. And mass production would become a fundamental aspect of American industry, setting a pattern of abundance for 20th century living. It wasn't just a transformation in how cars were built; it was a transformation in how all products were made.

Henry Ford invented none of this, but he was the first to fully embrace the methodology, and therefore the first to reap its benefits.

The moving assembly line placed the Model T in a class by itself. Already the car was the most practical and affordable on the market. Now, because it was able to produce so many of the vehicles in such a short period of time, and at such a low cost, Ford was able to drop the price even further. By 1915 a Model T could be purchased for as little as $440 (by the end of the 1920s the price tag would fall to $275). No other manufacturer could come close to matching that figure. Ford's profit margin on each automobile naturally shrank, but total volume increased significantly. The bottom line: more money for the Ford Motor Company.

And more cars on the road.

Because of its availability, the Model T was instrumental in reshaping American society. To many people it was nothing less than the great emancipator. Eventually, there would be problems: traffic jams, pollution, accidents. For now, though, it seemed a blessing.

"People no longer had to live within the shadow of the city," says Richard Scharchburg. "They no longer had to virtually live within walking distance of their work. They could commute. They could go live in places that were not served by streetcars. It improved all kinds of things.

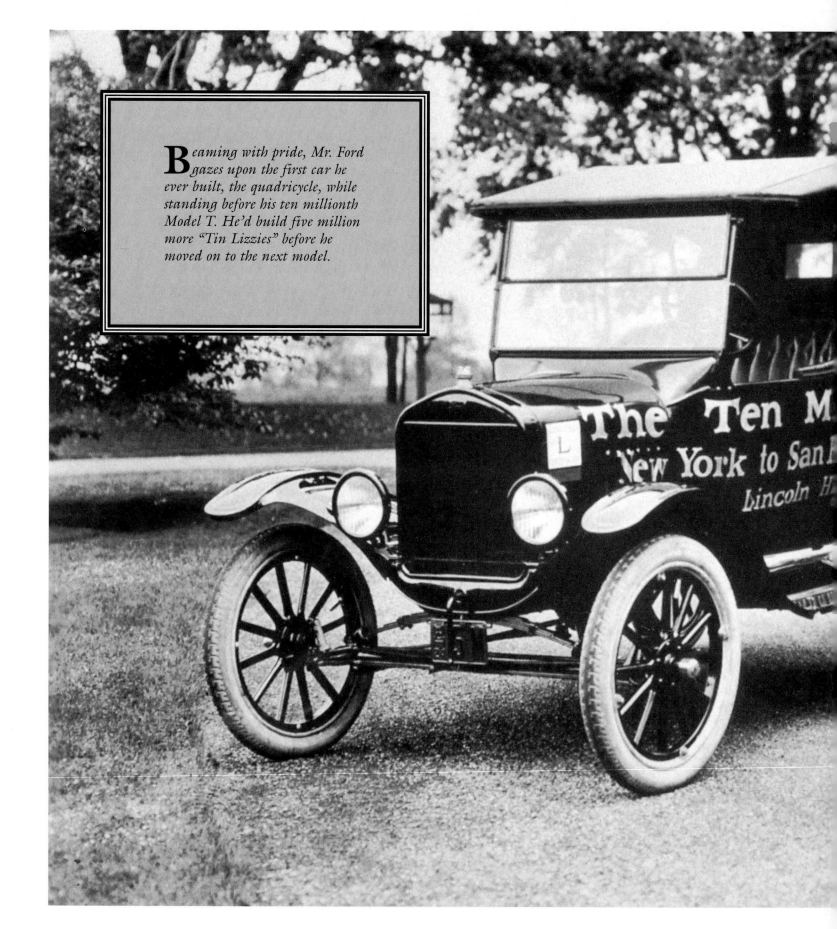

Beaming with pride, Mr. Ford gazes upon the first car he ever built, the quadricycle, while standing before his ten millionth Model T. He'd build five million more "Tin Lizzies" before he moved on to the next model.

Education, for example. Just think for a minute of the impact that the automobile had on education. All of these distinctly mediocre country schools—they could do away with them. Children could be transported to the city to attend better high schools."

Moreover, because the automobile increased the speed and frequency of delivery, it helped improve the quality of the food that people were eating; it was available to them in better condition. Physicians, too, were enamored, for they were able to make more house calls than was possible in a horse and carriage.

The automobile was also credited with no less an accomplishment than improving the quality of the species, for the range of cross breeding between different people was extended from approximately 30 miles (the radius of the horse and buggy) to a much larger sphere of interaction. Culturally, the automobile was also a boost. Civic functions and artistic functions—museums, galleries, theater performances—were suddenly accessible to people who lived in rural areas. They could drive in from the countryside and take advantage of cultural activities that had previously been out of their reach.

"I wouldn't say at all that the automobile had a dilatory effect on civic responsibility or civic involvement," says Richard Scharchburg. "For people living outside the central city, it enriched that portion of American life. It provided a relief from isolation."

Indeed, the automobile opened up a whole new world to a large segment of the population. It was an equalizer, capable of breaking down, at least temporarily, any number of social and economic barriers. "Farmers could get to town and buy the same kinds of clothing and they couldn't be distinguished," Richard Scharchburg says. "There was less discrimination based on the fact that the farmer had to go in his tattered overalls and crazy looking, worn straw hat. As the century began to wear on, often you couldn't tell a farmer except maybe by his tanned face below the line where his straw hat was. And, of course, his cal-

(Above left) Ford prided himself on building a car the "masses" could afford, especially his own workers, with whom he's pictured here aboard a 1913 Model T.

(Above) Teddy Roosevelt campaigns for his Bull Moose ticket atop a classic Model T: the era's most popular president aboard the era's most popular car.

(Far left)…Ridin' in style!

(Left) The Studebaker Press Car for the 1909 Glidden Tour.

Glad to see you any time.

It is not right for trees to grow so near the road!

LOVE IS BLIND.--

Florida Tourists.

(Above) Packards were a favorite of dignitaries and heads of state; This 1907 Packard Thirty with an extended wheelbase and luxury limousine coachwork gave one an air of importance, and it's not hard to see why. (Opposite page) Woodrow Wilson celebrating the end of WW I with the people of Boston on a Cadillac Model 55 limousine.

loused hands. But he looked less like a farmer."

To help fulfill his own prophecy of automobile ownership for the masses, in 1914 Ford made the astounding decision to double the wages of his employees. Ford Motor Company workers who had previously made approximately $2.30 a day would now make $5 a day. It was a stunning move, and one that fostered more than a little resentment within the industry. Henry Ford was accused of spreading labor unrest—after all, it was only reasonable to presume that workers at other companies would become jealous of their Ford counterparts.

Not that Ford cared. He wanted to attract the best workers to his plant—and keep them.

(Assembly-line work was so rigorous that turnover in the automobile industry was extraordinarily high—400 percent annually at Ford in 1913.) To do that he had to offer the highest wages. An equally important factor in his decision, though, was a desire to expand the market for his cars. In short, he wanted Ford workers to buy Ford automobiles.

"Henry Ford felt that the workers, as well as the stockholders and the consumers who benefited from lower prices, should share in the prosperity of the Ford Motor Company," notes David Lewis. "So he doubled wages overnight while reducing the work day by one hour (to eight hours). It was the greatest event in the history of wages and will

The unprecedented scale of Ford's River Rouge plant in Dearborn, Michigan still boggles the imagination. Here, parked out in the testing ground, is a single day's production: one thousand assembled chassis. (Opposite page) The engine assembly is tested in the Highland Park plant in Detroit.

remain so until some other big company comes along and overnight doubles wages and reduces prices and still makes a lot of money in the process. I don't think we should hold our breath."

Upon hearing of Ford's plan, workers from around the country descended upon Detroit, but only a fraction were hired. Long lines formed each day outside the Ford plant; frustration eventually led to periodic rioting. The strategy worked marvelously, though. Turnover at Ford dropped dramatically, to just 37 percent a year.

Meanwhile, many of the cities in the Midwest—home of the steel, auto, and rubber industries—were experiencing unprecedented growth. Vast numbers of foreign immigrants and African Americans from the South migrated in search of jobs. As unpleasant as assembly-line work could be, for many rural blacks who had toiled as sharecroppers and for immigrants who had worked in sweatshops, it seemed a reasonably attractive

Frederick Taylor had emerged as the philosophical father of the second American industrial revolution in the 1890s. Obsessed with efficiency, he pitted workers' physical actions against the stopwatch. In experiments with common laborers, every task was studied with the objective of reducing movement and thinking to a minimum. Workers became part of the machinery itself—industrial automatons who repeated the same action over and over again. It was oppressive and inhuman, and it worked. Taylor registered a 400% increase in productivity.

Michael Penland
Documentary screenwriter

alternative. As they flooded into Detroit, the number of workers in the auto industry increased from 15,000 in 1910 to 160,000 in 1920.

Those workers who landed jobs at the Ford Motor Company found their boss to be more than simply a benevolent millionaire who wanted his employees to be happy and well-fed. Henry Ford's popular image as a great American philanthropist was supported by his willingness to set up trade schools and English classes for his work force, and to sponsor company outings. He hired more African American workers than did any other automaker.

Even though he was one of the most powerful men in the country, Henry Ford could still find time to carve his wife Clara's initials in a tree on his estate. (Insert) Henry caught in a rare quiet moment with his son Edsel.

But there was a price to be paid. Ford expected his employees to share his views on everything and to adhere to a lifestyle that he deemed appropriate. Henry Ford believed in Americanism and in the individual's ability to "remake" himself. This wasn't surprising, considering Ford's background. He was a Midwestern farm boy who had risen to a place of prominence in the most lucrative industry in the world. He knew better than most that anything was possible.

At the same time, Henry Ford was a mass of contradictions. He practiced diversification, but only to the extent that it suited his needs. For example, he actively supported the hiring of black workers, but was unabashedly anti-Semitic. And his efforts to cleanse the great unwashed were often marked by condescension and authoritarianism. To mold people into his image of proper Americans, Ford established a "Sociological Department," which would not only teach employees English and advise them on financial matters, but also make recommendations on how to conduct their personal lives. Factory signs warned that no Ford employee was allowed to drink beer, wine, or liquor—even at home. Sociological Department investigators occasionally visited workers in their homes; they handed out a pamphlet entitled "Rules of Living," in which employees were encouraged not only to be wise with their money, but to use plenty of soap and water and not spit on the floor. Employees' wives were advised not to take in boarders; in this way they would avoid the temptation of illicit sexual encounters while their husbands were at work.

In general, the Sociological Department was run in a benign fashion by men with good intentions. "But this paternal practice began to suffocate some people who, as new Americans, were individualistic and disliked being told what to do and what not to do," says David Lewis. "Ford threatened to take away that big increase brought about by the five-dollar day if people didn't measure up."

By turns thoughtful and tyrannical, Henry Ford was a man who needed to be in control of his company and work force. If he was generally quiet and reserved, he was also an inflexible man prone to occasional fits of temper. In 1912, for example, when he returned from a trip to England, Ford discovered that a few of his top employees had decided to create a prototype for a new stream-lined version of the Model T, complete with dozens of refinements intended to broaden its appeal. They succeeded in surprising the boss, but not in pleasing him. Ford circled the car quietly several times before erupting madly. He ripped off one of the doors, smashed the windshield with a crowbar and stomped on the hood and roof. When he was through, the car was unrecognizable and a

clear message had been sent: No one was allowed to tamper with the Model T—not without first consulting its creator. Henry Ford had laid the groundwork for the modern automobile industry, but an increasingly myopic point of view, coupled with an unwillingness to adapt, ensured that the full promise of his accomplishments would be realized by his competitors.

Tunnel vision was not a problem for William Durant. As economic historian Dana Thomas wrote, "Durant was drunk with the gamble of America. He was obsessed with its highest article of faith—that the man who played for the steepest stakes deserved the biggest winnings." To loosen

Oldsmobile 14th Year

The Limited *started* right

Here is a brief, "inside" history of the most remarkable high-powered, six-cylinder automobile ever produced.

In 1906 we made plans to build an Oldsmobile "Six" which should be actually superior to all existing types, in touring comfort, speed, silence and reliability.

In 1907, after exhaustive shop tests, the first car was completed and road tests began. In 1908 an officer of the company drove a finished car many thousand miles.

In the course of these try-outs, the running gear received as much consideration as the motor. It was found that, within certain limits, the larger the diameter of wheels and tires, the more luxurious were the riding qualities.

In 1909 regular deliveries to the public were made. Then the wheel diameter was increased and the famous 42-inch tires became the standard equipment. The output was over-sold. Veteran motorists were amazed at the riding qualities revealed

by the large tires. Ruts, bumps and cobble-stones seemed to disappear by magic. Record high mileages were secured, sometimes treble the previous average.

The Limited of today, with its wonderful, long stroke motor and a multitude of improvements and refinements, is far ahead of the Limited of 1907. By the same token, it is ahead of other six-cylinder cars.

Although the seven-passenger touring car now runs on 43 x 5 inch tires, it is designed so skilfully that body, bonnet and wheels are in proper artistic proportion. The center of gravity is low, entrance and exit are made easy, and all the lines are graceful and pleasing.

While daringly original five years ago, the principles of its construction were sound, so we may say that—

The Limited started right, has been perfected to the utmost—and is today without serious competition.

Touring, Tourabout, Roadster and Limousine bodies. Prices, $5000 to $6300. The Oldsmobile catalogue describes all styles of the Limited, the Autocrat and the Defender. Sent gratis.

OLDS MOTOR WORKS, LANSING, MICHIGAN
Branches in the Principal Cities   Copyright 1912, Olds Motor Works   Dealers from Coast to Coast

---

entice Ford to join the fold. It was the second time he had made such an overture. Prior to the birth of General Motors, Durant had attempted to form a conglomerate that would have included Buick, Reo, and Ford. But Ransom Olds and Henry Ford had each demanded $3 million, and the deal fell through. Now, of course, the Ford Motor Company was worth considerably more, so Durant extended an offer of $8 million. Ford agreed, on one condition: he wanted the money up front...in cash. That proved to be a major stumbling block, for few of Durant's assets were liquid. Banks, fearing that he was already overextended, refused to lend Durant the money, and Ford remained an elusive quarry.

Within a year GM had serious cash-flow problems; expansion had come too quickly, and the company's successful divisions were incapable of sustaining its weaker divisions. William Durant was in deep trouble. In the fall of 1910 banks from New York and Boston rescued General Motors, but demanded that Durant give up control of the company.

William Durant was an optimist, though. Once, when asked if he thought the automobile market was reaching the saturation point, he reportedly said, "There is no such thing as saturation. When American mothers stop having baby boys, then the market will reach saturation." That attitude helped Durant stage a remarkable return to power just five years after his dismissal. In his absence, however, General Motors had undergone significant changes. Walter Chrysler, who was instrumental in the transition from wood frames to all-metal bodies in automobile production, had signed on as head of the Buick division. And another associate, Charles Kettering, invented the self-starter, one of the most important technological advances the automobile had seen.

With the death of the hand crank starter, the automobile suddenly became a simpler, safer mode of transportation. Nearly everyone who owned a car had something unkind to say about the crank. At best it was temperamental; at worst, dangerous. Now, brute strength was no longer required. The threat of suffering a broken jaw

Ford's stranglehold on the market, Durant decided that his company would be all things to all people. Yes, like Ford with the Model T, he would produce a car for the masses, but he also would produce cars for a more well-heeled audience. "An empire of cars for every purse and purpose," Durant said. And thus was born the concept of General Motors.

Durant filed incorporation papers in September of 1908, just as the Model T was taking the country by storm. He then undertook the task of constructing an empire of his own, with Buick as the foundation. Durant's first acquisition was Oldsmobile, which he financed with $3 million in GM stock and less than $20,000 in cash. He soon added Oakland (which became Pontiac) and Cadillac; within two years more than a dozen automobile and truck manufacturers fell under the General Motors umbrella. In 1909 Durant tried to

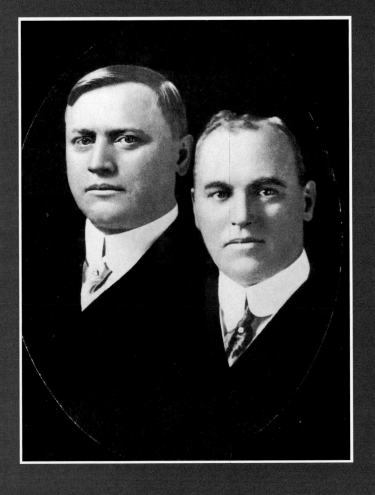

(Above left) The Dodge Brothers (circa 1910) made a formidable negotiating team: the tough but fair-minded John (left) loyally backed up by ex-deputy sheriff Horace (right)—a kind of good cop/bad cop routine with an automotive twist.
(Above right) A young William Knudsen when he first came to work for the Ford Motor Company (circa 1915). He became a top Ford executive before defecting to GM and finally the top spot in Washington directing war production for Detroit car makers.
(Right) Louis Chevrolet driving a Sunbeam in 1916.

VALVE-IN-HEAD MOTOR CARS

For all weather—For all purposes There's a Buick for all the Family

For winter driving over snowy streets; for cross-country touring; if a big car is needed or a small car desired, there is a Buick to fit your requirements. From six hundred-fifty to eighteen hundred dollars.

The Buick 7-passenger Sedan is a perfect family car. It has the beauty and luxury of a limousine, but does not require a chauffeur. It has the comfort and convenience of an electric, yet has a mileage range that is unlimited.

Closed and warm on the coldest winter days, an ideal town car for social or business purposes—the windows open all around make it cool and airy for touring in the hottest weather.

The strong, expertly constructed chassis and the powerful, economical valve-in-head, six-cylinder motor, are only a few of the superior features which make the Buick Sedan a car of notable value.

The Buick Six-Cylinder Sedan $1800

This model is also built in a three-passenger coupe, $1425.

THE BUICK MOTOR COMPANY
750 WOODWARD AVE.

from a recoiling crank starter disappeared. This gave the self-starter universal appeal, but made it especially popular with women, who became the fastest growing market for the automobile. Even Henry Ford, a male chauvinist at heart, authorized publication of a pamphlet directed at the burgeoning ranks of female drivers: "*No longer a shut-in, the new woman reaches for an ever wider sphere of action. And in this happy change the automobile is playing no small part. It has broadened her horizon, increased her pleasures, given new vigor to her body, and multiplied tremendously her range of activity. It is a real weapon in the changing order.*"

As historian Virginia Scharff points out, "Women motorists made a conspicuous cultural statement about female assertiveness. Donning goggles and dusters, wielding tire irons and tool kits, and taking the wheel, they announced their intention to move beyond the bounds of woman's place."

It was a rapidly changing world William Durant sought to conquer—again. In 1910 he hired a Swiss race car driver named Louis Chevrolet, who had been the star of the Buick racing team. Durant's instructions were simple: design a new car. Unfortunately, the two men did not exactly agree on the car's specifications. Durant wanted to challenge Ford and the Model T; he wanted a car for the masses. Chevrolet had something else in mind, something more…exquisite.

"Durant actually had several fights, verbal fights, with Louis Chevrolet over what kind of a car they were going to produce," says Richard Scharchburg. "Louis Chevrolet wanted the fine car, the mechanically fine, speedy car. Chevrolet, for example, was so proud that you could put a glass of water on the fender of his 1911 Chevrolet Classic Six, and it wouldn't fall off. You know, running the ball bearing or something over the car was nothing new to advertising in the auto industry."

The Classic Six was a wonderful car indeed. Unfortunately, at a cost of more than $2,100, it was hardly a vehicle for the common man; it certainly wasn't going to supplant the Model T. But by 1915 the Chevrolet operation—which featured a pair of sturdy, reasonably priced cars (the Baby Grand and Royal Mail)—had brought Durant over one million dollars in profits. He was back in the game! For the next few months he acquired huge blocks of General Motors stock, and by the fall of 1915 Chevrolet owned a majority interest in GM. The two giants then merged, once again leaving Durant at the helm of an automotive empire consisting of Buick, Cadillac, Chevrolet, Pontiac, and Oldsmobile—the same five divisions that constitute GM today.

Louis Chevrolet, meanwhile, found little joy in the success of the company that bore his name. He and Durant had split prior to the acquisition of General Motors. Like David Buick, Chevrolet could only watch as others profited hugely from his name.

For all his resilience and creativity, William

Durant remained a flawed, impulsive businessman. In time he alienated many of GM's top employees. Charles Nash resigned as president in 1916, shortly after Durant regained complete control. And in March of 1920, after a heated argument, Walter Chrysler walked away. Their final dispute was overheard by Alfred P. Sloan, who would later replace Durant as president of General Motors. "I remember the day," Sloan noted. "He banged the door on the way out, and out of that bang came eventually the Chrysler Corporation."

The next year, with GM reeling from the effects of a post-World War I recession, William Durant was once again pushed out of the company. Unfazed, he leaped right back into the automotive business, forming Durant Motors a mere six weeks after leaving GM. But he failed in that venture, too. Sadly, but perhaps inevitably, Durant's fortune faded, and in the latter stages of his career he tried his hand at operating a supermarket and a bowling center.

The Ford Motor Company, meanwhile, continued to chug along. Henry Ford owned half the U.S. car market in 1915, and among his greatest pleasures was the knowledge that many of the men who worked for General Motors drove Model Ts, for the Tin Lizzie remained the most affordable and popular automobile in the country. In 1919 construction was completed on the sprawling River Rouge plant, where the Ford

Women motorists made a conspicuous cultural statement about female assertiveness. Donning goggles and dusters, wielding tire irons and tool kits, taking the wheel, they announced their intention to move beyond the bounds of woman's place.

Virginia Scharff
Historian

work force would eventually reach more than 120,000. The Rouge, which covered 2,000 acres and boasted the longest assembly line in the world, was the hub of Henry Ford's industrial empire, as well as a monument to the man himself. Iron and coal arrived on his private boats, fresh from excavation in his own mines. Rubber was imported from a Ford-owned plantation in Brazil. Wood came from trees harvested on Ford land. The Ford Motor Company had become the largest privately owned company in the world.

"When you look at the Rouge plant now it conjures up the same sense of larger-than-life size as the pyramids must have thousands of years ago," says Harley Shaiken, an industrial sociologist who once worked as a machinist in Detroit. "There are other large factories today, but perhaps none quite like the Rouge. When the Rouge was first built, the world had never seen anything remotely like it. The Rouge redefined scale."

It also was in 1919 that Henry Ford rid himself of outside interference by buying out all of his minority stockholders, including John and Horace Dodge. The Dodge brothers had financed their own company in 1914 with dividends from the 2,000 shares of Ford stock they held. But they, like many other Ford Motor Company stockholders, were unhappy with Ford's insistence on channeling profits back into the company. The buyout cost Ford more than $105 million, but it gave him what he had always wanted: complete autonomy.

By the middle of the twenties, auto racing had reached epidemic proportions. Here, motor cars are lined up somewhat haphazardly before the start of the tour—but the excitement is contagious.

Auto-Races

BIG CARS
SUN. MAY 26
WILLIAMS GROVE SPEEDWAY
GEN. ADM. 50¢

(Above) Tours became a popular way to promote the early automobile. In this 1907 Chicago Reliability Run, most motor cars carried crews with them to assist in all possible emergencies.
(Below and right) Three views of the Stutz Bearcat. Touted as "the car that made good in a day," it was the first affordable sports car and a favorite of playboys during those carefree days before America entered the Great World War.

CHAPTER 3

Going In Style

The endless parade of cars streaming off Detroit's assembly lines in 1920 faced an increasingly annoying obstacle: mud. The majority of roads in the United States had been designed for equine use and were thoroughly unsuitable for automobile traffic. A congressional study undertaken in the first decade of the century revealed that only 150,000 of the country's two million miles of roads were surfaced. And most of those were merely covered with a layer of gravel (as

The 1931 Chrysler Imperial Series CG Convertible Sedan. Introduced in 1931, the Imperial was powered by the largest version of Cadillac's first eight-cylinder engine. Though greater in size than standard Cadillacs, it shared their new styling. The 5,000-pound Imperial could reach a top speed of 95 miles per hour.

GOING IN STYLE • 63

opposed to concrete or macadam).

With nearly 500,000 cars on the road by 1910, America needed better streets and highways, and not just for leisurely Sunday afternoon jaunts through the countryside. On a much more practical level, roads made impassable by mud were costing the rural government mail service $28 million each year. Farmers used the Model T as an all-purpose tool—running cider presses, saws, water pumps—but when it came to making a trip into town to purchase supplies, they angrily discovered that the automobile was useless without a dry road on which to drive.

"The automobile industry itself wanted better roads," says David Lewis. "There was a better roads movement. It was headed by Henry Joy, the president of Packard, and Henry Ford actually did not contribute as much as people hoped he would. But the people in various communities insisted on better roads as they acquired cars. And so the nation's highway network arose as the automobile got onto the roads."

The first mile of concrete highway was poured in Detroit in 1908, but it would be several more years before the federal government jumped on the bandwagon. Ford Motor Company produced films to publicize the need for highway construction, and in 1919 Army Major Dwight D. Eisenhower—in a hyperbolic attempt to dramatize the connection between better roads and national security—led a convoy of military vehicles on a cross-country trip from New York to San Francisco. It took three months to complete the journey, and thus was born a public works movement that would eventually result in the paving of 10 percent of the American landscape.

In 1921 the first Federal Highway Act was passed. It directed the Bureau of Public Roads to concentrate on "such projects as will expedite the completion of an adequate and connected system of highways, interstate in character." Proper financing, combined with advances in technology

(Above) By the 1920s, the motor vehicle industry had transformed Detroit into a bustling metropolis, as evidenced by the above street scene. (Below) Gas station with its "auto fountain" (circa 1930) in Bennettsville, S.C.

and engineering, brought rapid change. Total road mileage increased by only about 3 percent in the 1920s, but the number of roads that were either resurfaced or repaired doubled. Also changed was the system of highway numbering. East-west routes were assigned even numbers; north-south routes were assigned odd numbers. To the motorist, this was a marked improvement over the incomprehensible network of signs and arrows that previously dotted the landscape.

Better highways, the moving assembly line, and the closed car (which went from a 10 percent share of the market in 1919 to 90 percent in 1929) all contributed to the "car culture" of the 1920s. The U.S. became a society based on mobility and mass consumerism, with the automobile at its core. As people left the cities and took up

sive way for families to see the country. For those who wanted to travel, but found no great romance in communing with nature, roadside motels provided a warm, if somewhat unsavory, alternative.

Americans fell in love with their cars; sometimes they even fell in love *in* their cars. The advent of the automobile changed forever the nature of courtship. Young couples once restricted by circumstance to the parlor or front porch suddenly had access to freedom…and privacy! If this pleased a great portion of the population, it also was a source of anxiety to parents across the land. And while many automobile manufacturers viewed sex as a way to market their product (a trend that would reach its peak in the 1950s, but continues today), at least

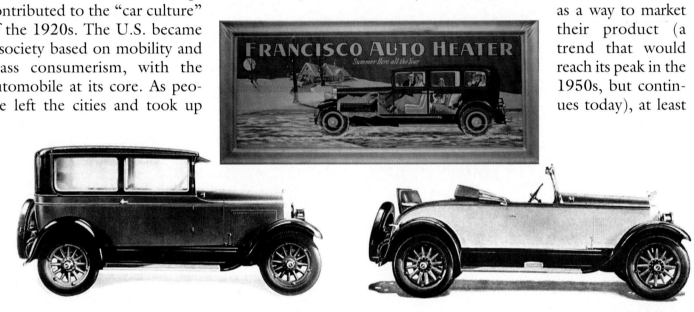

The Packard factory was a busy place during the height of the twenties. Packard remained a great name until the Depression forced it to attempt, unsuccessfully, to build economical cars. (Opposite page) This handsome 1927 Pierce-Arrow 36 features headlights that grow smoothly out of the fender, two spares in back, the distinctive hood ornament, and a woman driver.

residence on the edges of towns, not only were they giving birth to the first suburbs, they were also fostering a new, unregulated roadside culture. Retail districts popped up on the sides of highways. From coast to coast, billboards hawking everything from washing machines and vacuum cleaners to automobiles tempted the passing motorist. And, naturally, gas stations sprouted like weeds as the burgeoning middle class set out for the open road.

By 1922 autocamping had become a national fad (there were more than 15 million autocampers on the road), and became a relatively safe, inexpen-

one industry chieftain was notoriously prudish about such matters. According to popular legend, Henry Ford ordered that the back seat of the Model T be made uncomfortably narrow, thus discouraging amorous youngsters. Similarly, newspapers and cartoons routinely railed against the moral decay and godlessness supposedly represented by the new automobile culture.

Of course, their concerns were not entirely unfounded.

"The car changed the pattern of life," remembers John "Red" Cole, a former auto worker who came of age in the Roaring Twenties. "In the home or in the schoolyard, you might put your arm around a girl. But in the car you were captain in charge. And you tried to make a mate of the mate."

Of even greater concern were the Prohibition-era moonshiners who used souped-up Model Ts to smuggle whiskey on back roads (a phenomenon that later gave rise to stock car racing) and the bandits who discovered that it was much easier to make a clean getaway in an automobile than on horseback.

Generally speaking, though, Detroit wasn't concerned with how people were using its cars. So

Many of the elements that had made it popular—homogeneity, a lack of elegance and pretense—were now seen as liabilities. Once the ultimate middle-class car—a symbol of success—the Model T now became synonymous with professional and cultural stagnation.

It became a joke.

Meanwhile, the rest of the automobile industry was rapidly evolving. With the exception of the Ford Motor Company, innovation was everywhere. The 1920s was a difficult time for many small, independent car makers, but a fertile period

long as they were using them, business was good. Life was good.

Henry Ford's stubborn refusal to acknowledge the changing nature of the marketplace nearly proved fatal. The United States of the 1920s was a rich and ambitious place. Its consumers wanted more than functional transportation. They had money, and they wanted to spend it. They wanted their cars to reflect a certain image...a certain status. They wanted to feel rich. Predictably, the Model T began to suffer in this environment.

for some of the larger independents, including Packard, Willys-Overland, Hudson, Nash, and Studebaker. The most successful of the independents, though, were Errett L. Cord and Walter P. Chrysler.

Cord, a former race-car driver and salesman, was 30 years old in 1924, when he joined the Auburn Automobile Company in Auburn, Indiana.

He was a promotional wizard who not only turned the sagging company around, but also soon found himself at its helm. Unlike Ford, Cord understood the world in which he lived; he understood America in the 1920s. Cord's automobiles were much more than sturdy, reliable transportation. They were sleek and expensive. And extremely popular.

Once established in the business, Cord turned his attention to the Duesenberg brothers, Fred and Augie, who were best known for their prowess on the race track (their vehicles finished first at the Indianapolis 500 three times in the 1920s.) Cord acquired the company and hired the Duesenberg brothers to produce a line of passenger vehicles that would be the envy of the entire industry. And they did precisely that, first with the comparatively modest Model A Duesenberg, and, starting in 1928, with the lavish Model J.

Soon to become a favorite of movie stars and millionaires, the long, sleek Model J was an exquisite piece of machinery. And it was priced accordingly (actor Gary Cooper paid $14,000 for his "Duesy," an astronomical sum for an automobile in 1930). Lovely as the Duesenberg line was, it never turned a profit for E.L. Cord; rather, it came

As the twenties' economic boom continued, automobile manufacturers called upon Madison Avenue advertising agencies to craft "images" for their auto lines. (Right) A typical "bathing beauty" of the period confers her approval on the Lincoln Zephyr. (Below) A group visits the Grand Canyon in their 1924 Chrysler.

Former race-car drivers turned auto manufacturers, August and Fred Duesenberg (left) wanted to build great cars. With the help of Errett Lobban Cord (inset opposite) they made superb machines like the 1932 Duesenberg Convertible (above).

(Right) The 1931 Cord L-29 Convertible Coupe had an 8-cylinder, short valve engine, capable of delivering 125 horsepower. It was manufactured between 1929 and 1932 in Auburn, Indiana, the first front-wheel drive car to be produced in large quantities in America. The universal joint can be seen below the radiator grille. Elimination of a conventional drive shaft lowered the profile and allowed for sleek, rakish coachwork. Carl Van Ranst had worked on Indianapolis 500 cars before contributing to the design of the L-29. Unfortunately, few buyers were willing to purchase an unproven luxury car at the beginning of the Great Depression. Just 4,000 L-29's were produced. (Collection of Tom Evans.)

to symbolize the quality of his work. People who could not afford a Duesenberg would buy a Cord or an Auburn simply because they were produced by the man who made the Duesenberg. It was a shrewd and effective approach to business. By 1929, shortly before the Great Depression, Cord's fortune was nearly $30 million.

Walter Percy Chrysler's rise during the 1920s was even more dramatic than Cord's. Chrysler was a large man—figuratively and literally. Rough around the edges, with an enormous capacity for work and a tremendous zest for life, he had purchased his first car, a $5,000 Locomobile, in 1908, the same year Henry Ford introduced the Model T. Chrysler did not even know how to drive a car, but he was fascinated by the technology. "I did not simply want a car to ride in," he would later write. "I wanted the machine so I could learn all about it. These self-propelled vehicles were by all odds the most astonishing machines that had ever been offered to men."

Chrysler helped build steam locomotives for the American Locomobile Company in Pittsburgh before taking a job as manager of GM's Buick factory in Flint, Michigan, in 1912. By 1919 he was in charge of the Buick division, earning close to a half million dollars annually. By the time he left GM in 1920, he was financially set for life. Emotionally, though, Chrysler was adrift. He *needed* to be busy, a fact his wife, Della, recognized early in Walter's retirement. Annoyed by her husband's restlessness, she urged him to go back to work.

The automobile, of course, had a revolutionary effect on banditry. It simply aided the bandit tremendously. You know, it's very difficult to get away from a bank or train on horseback. But with the automobile, whoosh, away you go. It made the job, the occupation of the bandit much easier. Dillinger and Bonnie and Clyde, the movies, and Eliot Ness, of course, made the stories about the use of those cars legendary.

Richard Scharchburg
Historian

Walter needed little prodding. First, he unsuccessfully tried to help revive the struggling Willys-Overland company. Then, with the help of three young engineers, he revitalized the ailing Maxwell Motor Company. The Maxwell was a mid-priced car featuring a high-compression, six-cylinder engine and a stylish frame. But he wanted to introduce his new marque at the 1924 New York Auto Show, but was denied space because the car was not yet on the market. Chrysler was not so easily deterred. If the New York Auto Show wouldn't have him, then he'd stage a show of his own. He rented out space in the lobby of the nearby Commodore Hotel and put the Maxwell on display. The car soon became wildly popular, and by 1925 the Maxwell Motor Company had metamorphosed into the last of Detroit's Big Three: the Chrysler Corporation.

"Under an old car's shabby hood we had hidden the unsuspected power of our new high-compression engine," Chrysler would later write in his autobiography, *Life of an American Workman*. "Nobody had heard about a Chrysler car in 1923. But we had dreamed about it until, as if we had been its lovers, it was work to think of anything else."

Much as he loved that first car, the Chrysler Six, Walter Chrysler knew that diversity was the key to long-term success in the automobile world. He looked at Ford and saw a company choking on its own profits; a company afraid to make changes. Then he looked at General Motors, gliding along smoothly under the sure hand of Alfred Sloan, confidently producing cars for every taste and budget.

1926 Chevrolet Superior Roadster.
(Collection of Natural History
Museum of Los Angeles County.
Gift of Edward Baher.)

In Ford he saw the past; in GM he saw the future.

In order to effectively compete with either of the giants, Chrysler had to find a way to increase production quickly. Opportunity came in the form of an offer to purchase Dodge. Both of the Dodge brothers had died of influenza in 1920, and the company was later sold to a New York bank. In 1928 Chrysler acquired the Dodge name, its factories, and, perhaps most important of all, its nationwide network of dealers. One year later Chrysler unveiled two more marques, De Soto and Plymouth, both of which enhanced the company's rising stature in the automotive industry.

Still, keeping pace with General Motors in the 1920s was an enormous challenge, thanks mainly to the leadership of Alfred Sloan and the creative talent of Harley J. Earl.

Sloan, a graduate of Massachusetts Institute of Technology, joined General Motors in 1916, when his company, Hyatt Roller Bearing, was acquired by GM. Sloan became a rich man; he also found himself on management's fast track, and by 1923 he was running the largest industrial corporation in the world. Sloan was at once a shy marketing genius and a managerial wizard. He believed in fiscal restraint; thoughtful, detailed research; and teamwork. In fact, his implementation of a management system built upon the concept of shared decision-making was revolutionary in corporate America.

It was under Sloan that previously stodgy GM acquired a reputation for progressive thinking. *Styling* became fundamentally important. And with good reason. In the 1920s, as car ownership

in the United States tripled to almost 20 million, a pattern began to emerge. Instead of viewing the automobile as a once-in-a-lifetime purchase, the American consumer was starting to embrace the notion of "trading up." Henry Ford had either ignored or failed to recognize this sea change in behavior, but executives at GM—Alfred Sloan in particular—had not.

"If you were the first person in your town to have a Model T, that conferred an awful lot of status," says Harley Shaiken. "You could get somewhere. But once Henry Ford had created the situation where millions of people could get somewhere, then came Sloan's notion of how you defined and stratified those millions of people by the cars they drove.

"Ford was simply putting people on wheels. Once they got on wheels, Sloan had a vision of how to entice them into fancier wheels. Very few people identified with the Model T as a symbol in the way cars became a symbol many decades later. What was symbolic about the Model T was you could get anywhere virtually under any circumstances. If you wanted anything different than what Henry Ford was able to make at the lowest cost, you built it yourself. There was a huge upsurge of catalog business for accessories to the Model T. But Sloan felt you could put these accessories on in the factory. You didn't have to crank a Chevrolet, you could start it. You had a choice of colors. And the Chevrolet would lead you to another car, a Buick or an Olds, or ultimately a Cadillac. So Sloan redefined the market and thought of production; Ford thought of production and created a market."

SPORT PHAETON BY LOCKE

Commanding and powerful, yet with a distinct atmosphere of fleetness, the Sport Phaeton is a car of unusual attractiveness. A special moulding treatment and a flatly folding top accentuate the dignified sport lines of this body. The seat backs are high and at an angle which permits deep cushioning, providing exceptional comfort.

business, and under his guidance it developed a reputation for producing some of the finest custom-made automobiles in California. The Earl Automobile Works catered to the wealthy in general, and movie stars in particular. Earl's customers included Tom Mix and Fatty Arbuckle, who in 1919 paid a reported $28,000 for one of Earl's cars.

It wasn't long before word of Earl's daring design work reached Detroit. He was a bold and innovative stylist—a visionary who considered automobile design to be an art form. By the mid-1920s General Motors was warming to the notion

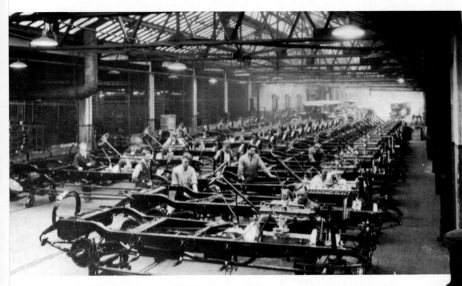

Packard factory, 1924. Despite the mechanical wizardry of the assembly line and mass production, the need for new models and the not-unrelated birth of planned obsolescence created the necessity of major factory retooling. This was particularly true at the Ford plant, where Henry Ford held on to the egalitarian idea of one car for every man or woman for a little longer than was financially sensible.

of planned obsolescence, but it needed someone with the confidence, imagination, and skill to bring the concept to life. It needed Harley Earl.

Likewise, Earl longed for a broader canvas on which to paint. So, when Lawrence P. Fisher, president of GM's Cadillac Division, offered Earl a position as a consulting engineer, Earl was quick to accept. His first car for General Motors was the 1927 La Salle, which was intended to fill a gap between the moderately priced Buick 6 and the high-end Cadillac. The car, with its soft, elegant lines, was warmly received by both automotive

critics and the buying public. Shortly thereafter, Harley Earl became a full-time employee of General Motors. But he was not just another executive. He was director of the company's newly created Art and Color Section—the first department in automobile history devoted exclusively to...*styling.*

In 1926 Ford offered the Model T in a choice of colors. But the public was unmoved. For several years Henry Ford had refused to heed the advice of those who could feel the winds of change. His son, Edsel, the company's president (albeit little more than a figurehead), along with most of his senior managers, had suggested dramatic changes in the Model T; perhaps, they said, it was time to replace the model altogether. To Henry Ford, of course, this was blasphemy. The Model T was like blood to him, and he would guard it with his life.

Eventually, though, Ford came to the realization that the Model T's time had passed. By 1926 annual sales were running nearly 30 percent below their 1923 peak. Henry Ford, as stubborn a man as

the automobile business had ever known, was forced to relent. The thought of dropping the Model T sickened him, but so did the thought of being outsold by General Motors. So, on May 25, 1927, the company announced that it was planning to unveil a new car to replace the Model T. Six days later the last Tin Lizzie rolled off the assembly line.

"Henry Ford felt that the Model T was the kind of car that Americans should drive," notes

It occurred to Sloan that if subtle changes in design and technology were introduced each year, and were supported by a shrewd and attractive advertising campaign, the average automobile owner would almost certainly grow dissatisfied with his current model. And, once lured to the showroom, he would be compelled to buy a new car. The concept was known as "planned obsolescence," and it became a cornerstone not only of the automotive industry, but of the American mass consumer society, affecting the way virtually all products—from lawnmowers to washing machines—were manufactured, marketed, and sold in the United States.

"If you can get people to give up their cars because they somehow seem outdated, because the new cars coming in look more fashionable, look more progressive, or have new kinds of styles and colors and contours, then that vehicle is as dead as if the engine had gone," says Bradford Snell, an author who has written extensively on the history of General Motors. "I mean, it is no longer of any use. And you've then created a new purchase. If you could make people discard still usable cars because they're somehow outmoded in terms of fashion, then you'd fantastically increase your sales in the automobile market."

Planned obsolescence was a stroke of genius. It effectively sold the illusion of progress by convincing the consumer that he could ascend the social ladder through the acquisition of material goods. And it helped General Motors supplant Ford as the dominant automobile manufacturer of the time.

Advertising was a critical component of planned obsolescence, for it was through carefully crafted media campaigns that the twin seeds of dissatisfaction and longing were planted. Early automobile advertising tended to be painfully dry, stressing the reliability of the product and the technical expertise of its manufacturer. By 1920, however, copywriters began taking a much different approach. They stressed style and design and power; the slightest change in appearance was trumpeted as nothing short of revolutionary. Some manufacturers embraced a lyrical approach to copywriting, in which their products were barely even mentioned. Instead, the ads focused on the positive—even heroic—traits of the company and, by extension, of the motorist who purchased the company's products. Among the more famous practitioners of this craft was Edward S. Jordan, who not only created the Jordan Playboy, but also the advertising campaign behind it. Jordan was a capitalist poet, as the following example illustrates:

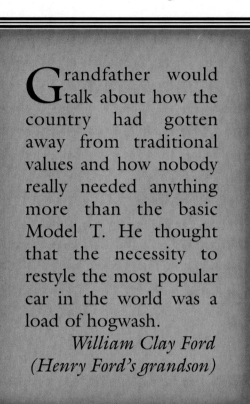

Grandfather would talk about how the country had gotten away from traditional values and how nobody really needed anything more than the basic Model T. He thought that the necessity to restyle the most popular car in the world was a load of hogwash.
William Clay Ford (Henry Ford's grandson)

"Somewhere far beyond the place where men and motors race through canyons of the town—there lies the Port of Missing Men. It may be in the valley of dreams of youth, or on the heights of future happy days. Go there in November when the logs are blazing in the grate. Go there in a Jordan Playboy if you love the spirit of youth. Escape the drab of dull winter's coming—leave the roar of city streets and spend an hour in Eldorado...."

Then, as now, the motorist was bombarded by advertisements intended to make him feel as though nothing could produce a more profound change in his life than the purchase of a new car.

"The buying public reflects an irrational attachment to the car that has deep historic roots nurtured by the (automobile) companies," says historian Ron Edsforth. "And the companies use this attachment—particularly the way the car is used to represent the self, the individual, to express something about the individual. The companies have used this successfully since at least the 1920s in order to sell automobiles."

Adds James Kunstler, author of *The Geography of Nowhere*, "The car represents a lot of other things in our national life. We have had a hard time making a distinction between physical mobility, the ability to go from point A to point B, and social mobility, the ability to rise socially and economically and to rise in the esteem of your fellow men."

Ford did not officially relinquish its position as the industry leader until 1927. The passing of the torch coincided with Harley Earl's arrival at General Motors. Earl, a native of Hollywood, California, was the son of J.W. Earl, a manufacturer of fine coaches and wagons who later founded the Earl Automobile Works. Harley Earl eventually entered the family business, and under his guidance it developed a reputation for producing some of the finest custom-made automobiles in California. The Earl Automobile Works catered to the wealthy in general, and movie stars in particular. Earl's customers included Tom Mix and Fatty Arbuckle, who in 1919 paid a reported $28,000 for one of Earl's cars.

It wasn't long before word of Earl's daring design work reached Detroit. He was a bold and innovative stylist—a visionary who considered automobile design to be an art form. By the mid-1920s General Motors was warming to the notion

Packard factory, 1924. Despite the mechanical wizardry of the assembly line and mass production, the need for new models and the not-unrelated birth of planned obsolescence created the necessity of major factory retooling. This was particularly true at the Ford plant, where Henry Ford held on to the egalitarian idea of one car for every man or woman for a little longer than was financially sensible.

of planned obsolescence, but it needed someone with the confidence, imagination, and skill to bring the concept to life. It needed Harley Earl.

Likewise, Earl longed for a broader canvas on which to paint. So, when Lawrence P. Fisher, president of GM's Cadillac Division, offered Earl a position as a consulting engineer, Earl was quick to accept. His first car for General Motors was the 1927 La Salle, which was intended to fill a gap between the moderately priced Buick 6 and the high-end Cadillac. The car, with its soft, elegant lines, was warmly received by both automotive

critics and the buying public. Shortly thereafter, Harley Earl became a full-time employee of General Motors. But he was not just another executive. He was director of the company's newly created Art and Color Section—the first department in automobile history devoted exclusively to…*styling.*

In 1926 Ford offered the Model T in a choice of colors. But the public was unmoved. For several years Henry Ford had refused to heed the advice of those who could feel the winds of change. His son, Edsel, the company's president (albeit little more than a figurehead), along with most of his senior managers, had suggested dramatic changes in the Model T; perhaps, they said, it was time to replace the model altogether. To Henry Ford, of course, this was blasphemy. The Model T was like blood to him, and he would guard it with his life.

Eventually, though, Ford came to the realization that the Model T's time had passed. By 1926 annual sales were running nearly 30 percent below their 1923 peak. Henry Ford, as stubborn a man as

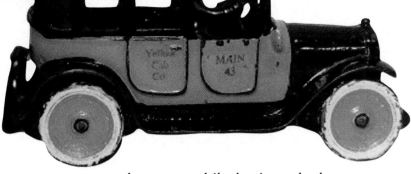

the automobile business had ever known, was forced to relent. The thought of dropping the Model T sickened him, but so did the thought of being outsold by General Motors. So, on May 25, 1927, the company announced that it was planning to unveil a new car to replace the Model T. Six days later the last Tin Lizzie rolled off the assembly line.

"Henry Ford felt that the Model T was the kind of car that Americans should drive," notes

The 1927 McFarlan Boattail Roadster was an attempt to lure middle-class comsumers. The straight 8 engine's output was rated at 80 horsepower. The styling of this model was so popular that it was sold as a replica model kit during the 1960s. (Collection of the Natural History Museum of Los Angeles County.)

David Lewis. "It was simple and dependable. It got them there, it got them back. What he didn't recognize is that other automakers were bringing out cars which did that and also were comfortable and offered many convenience factors. He simply held on to the car too long. It was one of the great mistakes of his life."

Production at Ford's massive River Rouge plant stopped as the company went about the laborious process of retooling for a new model. There was just one problem: no one had any idea what the new car would look like—including Henry Ford. The "official" word from Ford's executive offices was that an announcement would be forthcoming. The truth, however, was something else. Henry Ford had done the unthinkable. He had ceased production of the Model T without having a replacement waiting in the wings.

For the next six months the Ford Motor Company did not produce a single car. Meanwhile, Chevrolet, under the leadership of former Ford

THE NEW FORD ROADSTER

Smart, clean-cut, as speedy as it looks. A car for Youth and the Country Club. The windshield wings, as well as the windshield, are made of Triplex shatter-proof glass. Comfortable rumble seat can be installed in the ample rear deck at a small extra cost.

A bold new promotional scheme was launched along with Ford's new Model A—the "Roadster." Broad target marketing (clearly evidenced in this sales copy for "...Youth and the Country Club") and extra-cost options (rumble seat) are included with the obligatory sales pitch, "Smart, clean-cut...(and) speedy...." The auto industry was indisputably a pioneer in advertising as well as technology.

executive William Knudsen, saw its sales skyrocket. General Motors was one step closer to achieving Alfred Sloan's goal of crushing the Ford Motor Company.

Henry Ford was a survivor, though. And a clever one at that. His skill in the field of self-promotion was most evident in the months leading up to the introduction of his new car. While an admittedly large number of buyers were running to Chevrolet showrooms, many others were waiting to see what Ford had up his sleeve. He knew the public was starved for information about the car and was therefore careful to say nothing about it. Speculation in the press fueled even greater interest, and soon the rumors were rampant. Ford's "golden silence," as it has been called, was an effective marketing tool, and it cost the company

nothing. By imposing a news blackout, Henry Ford ensured that his new model would receive a ton of free publicity.

When the new car—dubbed the Model A—was introduced in late 1927, it was the most significant launch in the history of the automobile industry. Never before had a car generated such excitement. Ford began the campaign with a series of five full-page advertisements in every daily newspaper in the country. The first advertisement, signed by Ford himself, described the car's general features. The second and third advertisements discussed mechanical specifications and vowed that the car would be affordable. The fourth addressed the issue of appearance by including a photograph of the car (prior to its publication, no one had any idea what the Model A would look like). The fifth

The 1928 Ford Model A sported Lincoln-like styling and prices starting at $460. It also had a new kick under the hood: a 200.5 cubic-inch four that offered a capable 40 horsepower. Four hundred thousand were ordered in the first two weeks of its availability as a result of the marketing campaign and the assets of the car itself.

advertisement merely summarized the four previous advertisements.

Finally, the car was put on display. Ford threw open the doors to convention halls and dealerships across the country. Public reaction was overwhelmingly positive. People waited in line for hours just to get a glimpse of the new Model A. In some cases fights broke out and police were summoned. This, of course, led to even more news coverage, which led to more interest in the car. It was a fabulous cycle of publicity and it helped push sales of the Model A skyward; more than 400,000 orders were placed in the first two weeks alone.

"The Model A was one of the biggest news stories of the 1920s," says David Lewis. "It was comparable to Lindbergh's flight across the Atlantic or the Dempsey-Tunney fight or the Sacco-Vanzetti trial. In fact, it is one of the biggest industrial stories of the 20th century."

In retrospect, the Model A's initial success seems something of a curiosity. In both style and substance the car was clearly superior to the Model T, but it was hardly a groundbreaking vehicle; rather, it was an inexpensive, modernized version of its drab but reliable cousin. Novelty helped make the Model A the best-selling car in America in 1928, but Chevrolet's introduction of a new six-cylinder model in 1929 allowed GM to quickly recover. Within a few years, in fact, General Motors was producing 50 percent of all cars sold in the U.S.

Detroit had never known a year like 1929. More than five million cars were produced—a record that would stand for two decades. Mass consumerism was at its peak, and for virtually

every American, the automobile was at the top of the shopping list. As the suburbs grew and as businesses moved away from urban centers, the car was rapidly becoming a necessity. For many people, it was no longer a luxury; it was the single most important item in their lives.

Of course, not everyone could afford to pay for their new cars in cash. To accommodate this growing segment of the market, dealers in the 1920s strongly encouraged purchasing on the installment plan. The concept of buying on credit was not new; it had gained widespread acceptance some 75 years earlier, when Isaac Singer routinely extended credit in an attempt to increase sales of his sewing machines. In the early days of the automobile, only a dealer's most prized customers were permitted the luxury of short-term financing (typically, the buyer placed a down payment equal to or exceeding one-third of the purchase price, then paid off the remainder of the debt, with interest, over a period of one year). By 1925, however, the practice was becoming commonplace, with more than three-quarters of all new cars purchased on the installment plan.

"Henry Ford hated the idea of credit," says Harley Shaiken. "One of his values was that credit

The 1920s and 1930s saw a tremendous surge in the growth of companies that served the increasingly popular and affordable automobile. Credit departments made it easy to buy, service stations made gasoline easy to get and chains of repair shops made cars easy to fix, all while toy manufacturers captured the next generation of motorists.

The Cadillac for 1930

The 1930 Cadillac series 452 Phaeton came with the first 185 horsepower V-16, overhead valve engine (far right). With powerplants like these and styling to burn, Cadillac became the foremost producer of luxury automobiles in America. The Phaeton, which rolled on a 148-inch wheelbase was one of 54 semi-custom bodies offered by Cadillac's Fleetwood division. The rear compartment had its own small dashboard with a clock and speedometer as well as a second windshield which would be lowered by a hand crank. A total of 4,400 Cadillac V-16's were built from 1930 to 1940. (Collection of Joseph B. Runyan.)

was a bad thing. But Alfred Sloan sought to encourage people to buy cars by giving them credit, and in so doing redefined the American consumer society."

Henry Ford may have disapproved of the idea of going into debt to purchase an automobile, but the rest of the automotive industry (including Ford's dealers) did not. They recognized credit for what it was: big business. Across the country, dealers and manufacturers encouraged financing as never before. By 1929, on the eve of the Great Depression, nearly half of the nation's consumer installment debt of $2.9 billion was attributable to automobile purchases. It was not uncommon for people to mortgage their homes in order to buy cars.

"Consumer credit became more and more pervasive by the late Twenties," says Harley Shaiken. "It was a most magnificent high to buy things with money you didn't quite have yet. So installment buying, as many generations of Americans later found out, was a very easy thing to get into."

Inevitably, as the economy worsened, banks began foreclosing on personal loans and advising automobile manufacturers to stop extending unlimited credit. The Federal Reserve Board repeatedly pointed out the potentially disastrous consequences of the country's soaring consumer debt. By the end of the summer, the industry had fallen into a slump. The car-buying public was suddenly less impulsive. Caution became the order of the day. This was bad news for Detroit, where mass production soon led to over-

(Near right) The 1931 Ford Model A Coupe. The first Model A rolled off the assembly line in late 1927. It offered more comfort and performance than comparably priced cars and came in nine different models, ranging from the $500 Tudor Sedan to the $1,200 town car. By the end of 1930, Ford had sold four million Model As. (Collection of the Natural History Museum of Los Angeles County.)

(Far right) The 1931 Studebaker President Model 90 State Brougham was manufactured in South Bend, Indiana. Studebaker introduced its first eight-cylinder engine in 1928 on the upscale President Series. Their 132-inch wheelbase was the longest in Studebaker history. Subsequent Presidents had less formal streamlined bodies and lower prices which compromised their luxury status, but improved sales. (Collection of Darrell Dye.)

production, which the market could not absorb. After three decades of phenomenal growth, the automobile industry had, at least temporarily, achieved saturation. Buyers weren't buying. Investors were not investing. A legitimate crisis was on the horizon.

"During the Depression, installment credit came to a shrieking halt as the economy imploded," says Harley Shaiken. "People who were extended and who had extended themselves, in some cases, quite extensively, whether in the stock market or in terms of buying a car, all of a sudden saw the source of the income that was going to pay off the installment loans disappear."

While it would be simplistic to say that the automobile *caused* the Great Depression, it would be accurate to say that overextended credit played a significant role. And there is no overstating the impact of the industry's fiscal problems on the country as a whole. When Americans supported the automobile industry, they were supporting the oil, steel, rubber, and glass industries as well. The car was nothing less than a vehicle of prosperity for

the entire U.S. economy.

"The auto industry, by the end of the 1920s, was so intertwined with the fabric of economic life in America that when the auto industry started hitting the skids it would exacerbate the onset of the Depression in a major way," says David Lewis. "When installment buying choked up, and that affected car sales, it became not simply a downturn but a downward spiral that fed on itself; what was an economic downturn became a ditch."

Detroit was rocked by the Depression. New car sales fell 75 percent between 1929 and 1932. Payrolls were cut by 50 percent; the work force trimmed by one third. Although they suffered mightily, the Big Three weathered the storm better than the smaller independents, many of which disappeared completely. Gone from the marketplace were such familiar names as Cord, Stutz, Peerless, Franklin, and Pierce-Arrow.

And yet, brutal as the Great Depression was, it could not destroy America's transcendent love affair with the automobile. The luxury car market, ironically enough, reached a peak in the

early 1930s as Hollywood film stars in their custom-made autos provided the masses with a diversion from the harsh realities of the Depression. And while sales of new cars plummeted, ownership figures remained stable: two cars for every three people.

If Americans could not afford new cars, then they would cling to their old ones. The mass exodus of dust bowl farmers in their dilapidated Model Ts was seen as powerful and dramatic testimony to the appeal of the automobile as a dream machine. In some cases, families really would give up their homes before they would give up their cars. For a car, perhaps, could take them to a new place…to a new and better life.

I n the first years of the Depression, Detroit was hard hit. New car sales slumped an astonishing 75% between 1929 and 1932. Inevitably, the smaller companies went under. Ironically, however, it was during the Depression that the luxury car market in America reached its peak…While one quarter of America was out of work and on soup lines, Hollywood stars and their cars provided the kind of diversion the country was looking for.

Michael Penland
Documentary screenwriter

In the dust bowl, the car took on a new role as a life line—it became a home, the sole possession of many families. It was the wagon train of the great migration to the promised land of California. In fact, the Depression hardly made a dent in car ownership. There was still one car for each one and a half Americans. The difference was that they were now mostly used cars.

Ron Edsforth
Historian

CHAPTER 4

Labor Pains

For the automobile industry, 1933 offered a glimmer of hope. Car sales increased by more than 500,000 over the previous year (1932 was the low point of the Great Depression in Detroit), and figures would continue to improve throughout the rest of the decade. Other aspects of the nation's economy did not recover as quickly, perhaps because no other product was held in such high regard by the consumer. By 1933, after three years of limited automobile production, the nation's highways were becoming clogged with old, dilapidated cars. Even though fear and anxiety persisted, many people—especially in the middle class—finally decided to make the purchase they had been putting off. This, in turn, gave Detroit a significant boost: by 1935 automobile production was less than 10 percent behind the best years of the 1920s. It helped, of course, that the newly

This 1938 Packard factory features rows of the Packard Limousine, popular among the rich and famous.

Foster and Kleiser

WORLD'S HIGHEST STANDARD OF LIVING

There's no way like the American Way

The use of this Poster Panel donated by Foster and Kleiser Company

installed Roosevelt administration understood the link between a healthy auto industry and a healthy national economy and thus put people to work on a variety of public works projects, such as paving country roads and repairing bridges.

Despite this assistance, the independents were ill-equipped to handle the lean years. Packard and Nash survived the Depression, as did Willys-Overland and Studebaker. Overall, though, the influence of the independents was significantly weakened. By the end of the Depression years their share of the market had fallen to a mere 10 percent (from 25 percent in 1929).

Even as workers returned to the assembly lines and Detroit rebounded, a cloud of uncertainty hung over the automobile industry. Half of all employees had been laid off between 1929 and 1932, and those who retained their jobs were forced

In the face of major labor unrest over working conditions and pay, The National Association of Manufacturers sponsored this famous 1937 billboard (opposite page) as part of a national advertising campaign to deflect criticism and pump up Depression sales.
(Above) Working as migrant workers in California, refugees from Abilene say of home, "The finest people in the world live in Texas, but I just can't seem to accomplish nothing there. Two year drought, then a crop, then two years drought and so on."

to accept pay cuts and shorter work weeks. Antagonism between labor and management intensified. Speed-ups on assembly lines were common, making a difficult job almost unbearable. The time was ripe for unions to organize angry, unhappy workers. But the cost of that organization would be steep.

Management opposition was only one barrier to the formation of unions. The

Looking for work in the auto industry during the depression was very, very hard. Every day, the streetcars were full of thousands of people who would get off at the stop right outside the Ford plant and just get in line. I was one of them.

We used to put newspapers under our shirts, cause we had heard that a newspaper will keep you warm. And we stood in line for a long time and felt cold…real cold. And it wasn't easy, it wasn't easy. You stood in line all day and then a man comes over, and says, that's all for today. I stood in line ten days before I got hired.

And I had to slip somebody fifty dollars to get it done.

Espedito Valli
Retired auto worker

American Federation of Labor represented primarily craftsmen; assembly line workers in the auto industry did not easily fit under the AFL's umbrella. Nor did the workers themselves have any expe-

(By 1938 the work force at the River Rouge plant numbered 90,000. Nearly 10 percent of those workers had been coerced into serving as spies for the Service Department.) Bennett's army was an

Toughman Harry Bennett (left) was Ford's muscle in 1938, brutally enforcing the strict company policy, while Ford advertising (below) pretended everything was fine. Bennett was finally ousted by Henry's grandson, Henry Ford II, in a fierce power struggle.

An admired grace of line and

SEEING the new Ford as it speeds along the broad highway or parked proudly beside the Country Club, you are impressed by its flowing grace of line and contour. « « There is about it, in appearance and in performance, a substantial excellence which sets it character and position unusual in a low-priced car. « « « « « To women especially, its safety, its comfort, its reliability and its surprising ease of operation put a new joy in motoring. « « « « « « «

THE NEW FORD COUPE

rience in organized labor, a fact exploited by management at the Big Three.

At Ford, growing labor unrest proved a boon to the career of a man named Harry Bennett. A former boxer and sailor, with connections to the Detroit underworld, Bennett joined the Ford Motor Company in 1917, at the age of 24. Although on the smallish side, Bennett was a hard man prone to cruel and violent behavior—traits that, ironically enough, made him a highly valued employee in the 1930s. He accepted the ugliest jobs with glee. If a worker was causing trouble, Bennett took care of him; if someone had to be fired, Bennett fired him.

Eventually, Bennett assembled a cadre of watchmen whose responsibility was to maintain order at the River Rouge complex. They were the basis for the infamous Ford Service Department, a virtual secret police force that developed a network of informers on the shop floor.

The science of mass production: an interior shot of the labyrinthine Ford River Rouge manufacturing plant, shown here producing V-8 engines in the 1950s.

When You
BUY an AUTOMOBILE
You GIVE
3 Months' Work
to Someone

Which
Allows
Him to
BUY
OTHER PRODUCTS

BUY A CAR NOW—HELP BRING BACK PROSPERITY

vice. To Ford workers, it was the police state personalized in the form of Harry Bennett. And it wasn't service that was provided; it was fear and terror on a daily basis. You didn't know who was working next to you. You didn't know what you could say. You didn't know how you could act. If the foreman wanted you to cut his lawn over the weekend, you could hardly afford to say no before the Depression, and certainly not after the Depression.

"The Service Department brought fear in new ways on the job. After the Depression, it became much worse in Ford plants, because so many Ford workers were laid off. There was an endless supply of people without jobs who would take yours in a minute and everyone knew that. Under these circumstances, even to look the wrong way could be picked up by the so-called Service Department. So the service it provided was of unknown quantity to anyone who contacted it within the plant. What was provided that was known was the sense, literally, of terror."

The Ford Service Department was the Sociological Department

unsavory collection of thugs and ex-convicts who looked for troublemakers in general, and union activists in particular. So frightened were workers that during lunch breaks they would talk loudly and incessantly about sports and other trivial matters, lest anyone get the idea they were contemplating a labor revolt.

"Ford's Service Department really was about as misnamed an organization as one could imagine," says Harley Shaiken. "It did everything but ser-

run amok. There was nothing altruistic about it. Bennett and his goons patrolled the plant in menacing fashion, threatening to fire any employee who slacked off for even a second. Sometimes, when a man asked to use the bathroom, Bennett would follow him in and check the toilet afterward, to make sure that the man wasn't simply taking an unauthorized break. And if he happened to find the employee smoking in the bathroom, well, that person would not only be fired, he might receive a severe beating as well.

Similarly, the Service Department tried to monitor the behavior of employees outside the plant. If Bennett heard that a worker was drinking too much, or otherwise engaging in conduct deemed "inappropriate," a home visit would be in order. And, of course, a personal visit from Bennett and his hench-men was one of the worst things that could happen to a Ford employee.

"It was just like a military outfit," remembers David Moore, who worked at Ford in the 1930s. "They took direct orders from Harry Bennett and whatever Harry Bennett told them to do, they would do it. People were beaten, people were killed. People were just brutalized by the Ford Service Department. You had to work with one eye over the shoulder in whatever you were doing, because you never knew when you were going to be the next one, especially if you had been involved in any activity that the Ford Motor Company did not want you to be involved in, or wouldn't permit you to be involved in if they knew it. And you could not even talk to the guy working next to you. One individual was fired for just smiling. The Service Department of the Ford Motor Company was…I think you could compare it with the German Gestapo. They were the enforcers. They were the law in the Ford plant."

By the early 1930s Henry Ford's reputation as

The River Rouge plant represents a long history of suffering. A whole long history of people dying. A long history of people being denied, deprived of their manhood and dignity.

You worked at Ford's because two of the Big Three didn't hire blacks. Only Ford did. But the blacks had to pay a price at Ford. That price was the conditions in the foundry.

And the foundry was a hellhole. A deathtrap. To work in the foundry, you had to be an individual of great strength and determination. No other part of the plant had such conditions.

That's where all of the blacks were hired, including me.

David Moore
Retired auto worker

a philanthropist was justifiably eroding (The *New York Times* would dub him the "Mussolini of Detroit".) Conditions at the River Rouge plant were intolerable. And Ford himself was offering one tasteless observation after another, revealing in the process an insensitivity toward the working-class families who had been crippled by the Depression: "These are really good times, but only a few know it," he said in 1931; and, three years later, as millions tried to rebuild their lives, he added, "If you lost your money, don't let it bother you. Charge it up to experience."

Moreover, in a striking display of ignorance and anti-Semitism, he had once said, "Unions are organized by Jewish financiers, not labor. A union is a neat thing for a Jew to have on hand when he comes around to get his clutches on industry." Regardless of the opponent, Henry Ford knew who his allies were. Harry Bennett became Ford's most valued soldier in the battle between labor and management. True, he was sadistic. But he was also fearless. And loyal.

Bennett was at the center of the storm in March of 1932, when local Communist organizers led a "Hunger March" through downtown Detroit. The march, which drew several thousand participants, ended at the Ford Motor Company employment office, at the gates of the River Rouge in Dearborn. The protesters, whose stated goal

Edsel Ford (left) was Henry and Clara's only child, and he officially became president of Ford in 1918. Edsel was loyal and talented, yet his overbearing father found it impossible to fully relinquish power. Public disagreements (above) and private power struggles were common, and it has been said that Henry found Edsel to be "too soft."

was to hold Henry Ford accountable for the massive layoffs and cutbacks that typified the preceding three years, were met by members of the Dearborn Police Department and Ford security guards. The police used tear gas and fire hoses (it was a cold day, so the water froze on contact) to try to control the mob, but only succeeded in heightening hostilities.

When Bennett identified himself to the mob, he was pelted with bricks, prompting the police to open fire. By the time the battle ended, five demonstrators were dead, including a young man Bennett had pulled down on top of himself to use as a shield. Nineteen others were seriously wounded.

"The Hunger March took place because of unemployment," recalls David Moore. "People were unemployed. They had no jobs. Ford had promised that he would keep his plant open and that people would have jobs. The unemployment councils in the city of Detroit and all the areas around decided that they would march on Ford to see whether he would keep his promise or not. These were young men just in the bloom of life. And their lives were taken away from them within seconds, for no reason at all—just to demonstrate to the Ford Motor Company that we were willing to work."

Interestingly enough, the ugly denouement of the Hunger March was played out in front of a group of several dozen engineers from the Soviet Union. Henry Ford was held in high regard by Soviet officials, largely because they had been doing business together since 1928. Now, though, a Communist-led demonstration had been violently squelched by Ford's own men.

If this prompted any serious introspection on the part of Henry Ford, it wasn't immediately evident. Author Upton Sinclair, in a scathing indictment that parodied earlier criticisms of the Model T, wrote, "Ford cars come in any color—as long as it's the color of fresh human blood." A brutal assessment, but not without merit given the fact that the consequences of the Hunger March were most readily apparent in the form of a circle of machine gun towers erected on the perimeter of the River

Rouge. The orders came from Harry Bennett, whose sphere of influence was widening with each passing day.

"The Hunger March became a very powerful symbol of workers collectively challenging their condition," says Harley Shaiken. "But the response to the Hunger March defined an important part of the decade. It was met not with a pronouncement, not with a sense of listening to complaints, but literally with hoses and bullets. The dead and wounded galvanized the city and in a sense galvanized the nation."

Meanwhile, Edsel Ford, still the company's president, attempted to devote his time and energy to issues of engineering and design. He brought out the mid-priced Zephyr under Ford's Lincoln marque, and in 1937 introduced the Mercury. He also managed to fulfill a long-time goal by establishing a design department that would operate independently of the engineering division (General Motors, of course, had been doing this for years). In matters of labor and production, Edsel tried to be a reasonably progressive thinker, but often found himself at odds with his aging, autocratic father and the tyrannical Harry Bennett. Despite Edsel's best efforts, the Ford Motor Company continued to slip; by 1937 it owned less than one quarter of the U.S. auto market and had fallen to the bottom of the ladder among the Big Three.

The challenge facing Edsel Ford was immense. Throughout the industry, labor unrest was the issue of the day. The harsh economic conditions of the Great Depression fostered a powerful sense of worker solidarity, and when the National Labor Relations Act (which guaranteed the right to collective bargaining) was passed in 1935, beleaguered workers had cause to rejoice. Local unions previously governed by the AFL were absorbed by a new organization known as the United Auto Workers, which was aligned with the Congress of Industrial Organizations. The CIO had already been successful in organizing workers in the steel industry; but the auto industry had no intention of simply rolling over. A protracted battle seemed inevitable.

Flint, Michigan, was the home of the most celebrated strike in American labor history: The 44-day sit-down strike, when the auto workers, trying to organize the UAW during the CIO organizing period, sat in the General Motors plant, Fisher Body 1. And they sat in, some women, too, mostly guys, sat in for 44 days and 44 nights. I like to say they beat Noah in the ark by four days and four nights.

The whole world was aware of the strike, of this particular sit-down. And I interviewed Jenora who happened to have been one of the heroines of that strike. So as I asked this 82-year-old woman about that season '37, she suddenly becomes a girl again. "We won that fight. We were recognized. And that night was Mardi Gras. That night was liberation day. That night was New Year's Eve."

And then she fell back onto the pillow, and she says, "Studs, for crying out, this should be a better world than it is."

Studs Terkel
Writer

In 1936 the UAW trained its collective eye on General Motors. In part, GM was chosen precisely because of its stature; if the world's leading manufacturer of automobiles could be toppled, the reasoning went, then surely other companies would follow. Beyond that, though, there was the more practical matter of Ford simply being too tightly controlled. GM seemed like the logical place to begin.

A series of work stoppages and quickie strikes occurred with increasing regularity. But while they proved irksome to management, they were not fatal. Striking workers were instantly replaced and the lines rolled again. It became apparent to union organizers that more drastic measures would have to be taken. Somehow, production would have to be stopped for an extended period of time.

The solution was revealed on December 30, 1936, in Flint, Michigan, when first-shift workers at two GM Fisher body plants shut down the assembly line and locked the doors to prevent strikebreakers from entering the facility and taking their jobs. The American automobile industry was about to experience its first prolonged, organized sit-down strike.

"We had just come back from lunch," remembers Bruce Malotte, who worked at GM in 1936. "And we knew it was going to happen, but they'd told us to wait until we got the word. And about 45 minutes after lunch, they came down and said, 'That's all, shut her down!' And we just walked off the line. Of course, management kept that line just inching like that. They didn't shut it off. In case you wanted to work, you could get on there and show them that you weren't in favor of the strike. But I remember a guy came down the line. And he had a solder float—that's a file that weighs about a pound and a half, with a handle on it. And he just said, 'Get off of that line, or I'll roll your head down that aisle.' And everyone got off.

"Some of the older guys were scared to death that it would turn into a riot, or they would lose their jobs. But they didn't offer too much resistance. The majority of people were in favor of the strike."

Approximately 10 percent of the GM work force had already quietly enrolled in the UAW. Previously, they had been unable to publicly voice their beliefs; to do so would almost certainly have resulted in dismissal. Now, though, the union had leverage. Two Fisher body plants were shut down in Flint; a third, in Cleveland, was also

For many people who work in the industry the UAW means a lot more than a place where they pay dues. It's not just a union. It is something that has transformed people's lives. It's an institution that people gave their lives for.

When your grandfather was a member of the union, your father was a member of the union. There was a sense that this was an institution you turn to. In my grandfather's mind (the union) made working at Ford's tolerable in a way that it had never been for him before the union.

Harley Shaiken
Historian and
former UAW member

stopped by a strike. Others were soon to follow in Indiana, Missouri, and Wisconsin. Under these conditions, production was impossible. General Motors was paralyzed.

The company decided to fight the strike through legal channels (the Supreme Court would eventually determine that the sit-down strike was an unconstitutional tactic), and it soon won an injunction against the striking workers. The injunction was overturned, however, when it was revealed that the judge presiding over the case happened to own more than $200,000 in GM stock.

On January 11, 1937, 12 days after the strike had begun, General Motors, with the aid of the Flint Police Department, resorted to the use of force in an effort to remove the workers. Among the witnesses was Victor Reuther, a UAW activist, and the brother of Walter Reuther, who went on to become president of the UAW.

"When I reached Fisher Two I was met with shouts from the sit-down strikers on the second story saying, 'Dammit, Reuther, send us some food, and turn the heat on!'" Victor Reuther

recalls. "The corporation had shut off the heat, which they had allowed to stay on more to protect their machinery than the strikers. They had allowed food to be passed through since the day the strike began, and suddenly that was cut off, too. This was a warning to us that something serious was in the making."

Police officers armed with guns and tear gas quickly moved in and tried to regain control of the plant. Strikers retaliated with the weapons at hand. They sprayed the police with water from fire hoses. They stretched tire inner tubes between steel posts on the plant roof and fashioned sling shots; for ammunition they used rocks, bottles, and door hinges. When police fired tear gas missiles into the plant in an attempt to smoke the workers out, a group of sympathetic picketers (which included many women and children—

We knew that the world knew that our strike was on—and by God we were going to win it! We finally found a way to close down a big corporation and keep them closed down. And there was nothing they could do about it. Everything they tried, the union said, "No, we ain't agreeing to that," or, "We ain't going to do this," or, "We ain't going to do that." "When you get ready to agree to a contract, we'll come out of the plant." And when they finally did we knew right off the bat that we were going to get a little decent treatment from then on, although it took a long time before we finally got it around to that.

Larry Huber
Retired auto worker

relatives of the strikers) broke from the line and shattered as many plant windows as possible so that fresh air could reach the workers. But the fight was not over.

"The police started to drive past the opening of the building where the sit-down strikers were and firing directly in," Victor Reuther remembers. "And I wanted to block their movement. So I called upon the picketers to form a barricade of their own cars. My God, these were their life savings, but they took their own old jalopies and turned them over and formed a barricade so the

police couldn't get through. I think that saved many lives."

The "Battle of the Running Bulls," as the confrontation came to be known, ended with the police in retreat, but not before dozens of people had been injured, including many by police gunfire. It was a strong indication that not only were the striking workers willing to risk their lives, but that the people of Flint were supportive.

Michigan Governor Frank Murphy, a close friend of President Franklin D. Roosevelt, ordered the National Guard to assemble in Flint. Whether its mission was one of peace or violence was at first unclear. John J. Lewis, the founder of the CIO, suspected the Guard would be used to break the strike. If so, he promised the governor, "When your troops arrive, I will take my place with my brothers at the plant. And when they shoot they will pierce my body with their bullets." The governor, saying he had no intention of being remembered as "Bloody Murphy," put the troops between the strikers, the strike breakers, and local officials; their assignment, much to the chagrin of GM President Alfred Sloan, was not to evict the striking workers, but simply to prevent further conflict. Soon, heat was restored to the Fisher body plants, and the workers were allowed to receive food from the outside. There would be no more bloodshed; the dispute between labor and management would be settled at the bargaining table.

"We were tickled to death to have (the National Guard) there," recalls Bruce Malotte. "Because they were certainly on our side and they let us know it. They were not there to protect General Motors, but rather to protect the public. And we were the public."

On February 11, after a week of negotiations (with Governor Murphy presiding), a settlement was reached. The 44-day sit-down strike had led to GM's signing the first union contract in the history of the U.S. automobile industry. It was a stunning victory for the workers, the repercussions of which would be felt for generations.

"They literally seized the plants and organized that seizure in a way where it became a colossal test of wills between the largest industrial corporation in the world and a union that had yet really to establish itself," says Harley Shaiken. "It was too unequal for any sensible person to predict anything but a corporate victory."

The union next turned its attention to Chrysler, the nation's second-largest automaker. Once again, workers seized control of the plants, and once again friends and families formed picket lines outside (singing "Dollars from Chrysler" to the tune of "Pennies from Heaven"). This time, though, there was no violence. In April Chrysler settled with the UAW, and soon nearly every auto manufacturer in the country was at the bargaining table.

The notable exception was the Ford Motor Company, whose founder angrily proclaimed, "We'll never recognize the United Auto Workers union, or any other union." Henry Ford had never let his stockholders tell him how to run his company; he was not about to permit his own workers to do so. If it was a fight they wanted, he would give it to them.

On May 26, 1937, Walter Reuther, who had once worked on the Ford assembly line, led a group of UAW activists to the River Rouge. Reuther had obtained a permit to distribute union literature. As workers crossed an elevated footbridge that led inside the plant, Reuther, Richard Frankenstein, and other UAW organizers handed out pamphlets. There was nothing particularly threatening (or illegal) about this gathering, but Harry Bennett took it as a personal affront. He dispatched members of his Service Department to the gates of the Rouge. There, the union organizers were attacked and beaten. As Walter Reuther later wrote, "The men

Alfred P. Sloan Jr. led General Motors to industry dominance—but was also the first of the big three to submit to the United Auto Workers in 1937.

picked me up about eight different times and threw me down on my back on the concrete. And while I was on the ground, they kicked me in the face, head, and other parts of my body. And then they picked me up and threw me down a flight of stairs."

Others who were with Reuther, including a minister and a woman—volunteers who had agreed to help distribute leaflets—were the victims of similarly brutal treatment.

For once, though, Bennett's strong-arm tactics backfired. The "Battle of the Overpass" was captured by photographers, and the sickening images were reprinted in newspapers across the country. The photos—in particular one of Reuther and Frankenstein, both bloodied and beaten, comforting each other—became a symbol of Ford's arrogance and callousness. As it had during the Hunger March of 1932, the Ford Motor Company reacted with violence to an essentially peaceful demonstration.

"It shocked the American public into a realization that fundamental simple human rights were being denied workers, and Ford workers in particular," Victor Reuther says. "And it gave a moral shot in the arm to the CIO's efforts and UAW's efforts to organize Ford. It became a rallying cry around the world."

Resolution would take time, though. Ford held the union at bay for the next four years, even as he suffered health problems and his company endured a power struggle among Edsel Ford, Charles Sorensen, and Harry Bennett.

In April of 1941, workers staged a massive walkout after Bennett fired eight members of a grievance committee. Ford presumed he could rely on black workers to help him break the strike. But he was wrong. Encouraged by the support of

NAACP officials, the great majority of African Americans at the Ford Motor Company opted to join the union.

"When the strike started, some black workers in the plant had a lot of apprehension and distrust of the unions," remembers David Moore. "The unions themselves, prior to the Congress of Industrial Organizations, had never given the black workers a fair shake. And Ford tried to take advantage of that. But when the organizing drive started, there were promises made: 'If we organize, you're going to be part of this union. You're going to be in the leadership role of this union. You're going to get the same wages anybody else gets. You're going to get the same benefits.' And so a lot of blacks said, 'Well, let's give it a try.'"

On April 3 Henry Ford gave into pressure from Governor Van Wagners and from his son Edsel who had wanted to accept the union years earlier. Ford signed an agreement on June 20, 1941, one month after 70% of his workers voted for affiliation with the AFL-CIO. As with the $5 day, he did his competition one better and gave his workers the best deal among the big three.

Michael Penland
Documentary screenwriter

In May of 1941 the National Labor Relations Board gave Ford workers the right to hold a union election. More than 70 percent of the work force voted for affiliation with the UAW. Less than 3 percent of the membership opted for non-union status. Henry Ford, now in his late 70s and exhausted by the ceaseless fighting between labor and management, was so upset by the outcome that he vowed to shut down the plant, even though such a move would surely provoke rioting on a grand scale.

As it turned out, Ford did no such thing. In fact, on June 20 he signed an agreement with the union that gave Ford Motor Company employees the best contract in the automobile industry. The reason for such a dramatic change of heart? Clara Ford, Henry's wife, who threatened to leave him if he did not make peace with the union.

"I felt her vision and judgment were better than mine," he later explained. "I'm glad I did see it her way. Don't ever discredit the power of a woman."

"Union Official Beaten at Ford" was the headline for this startling image appearing in national newspapers across America on May 27, 1937. The Ford Motor Company had been resisting the United Automobile Workers union, which had secured a permit to distribute UAW literature outside the River Rouge plant. On May 26, 1937, the UAW attempted to do just that. The man with the coat pulled over his head is Richard Frankenstein, UAW organizational director, and the men pummeling him are Ford "Service Department" employees, whom Harry Bennett had instructed to "moderate" the situation. Sixteen people were reported injured—some severely—but the incident was powerfully advantageous to the union movement.

Meanwhile, in Hollywood...

In 1932 Clark Gable (above) proudly posed beside his ultra-rare Duesenberg SSJ (Short Supercharged) which could go 104 mph—in 2nd gear! With its 7-litre engine stuffed into a shortened wheelbase, only two were built. The other was owned by Gary Cooper. The "Duesy" is considered by many experts to be one of the great machines of all time.

(Far right, top) The lovely starlet Madge Evans graces the luxurious cab of a 1932 Packard Limousine.
(Far right) The automotive tastes of everyone in Hollywood were catered to—especially when the number one box-office draw for four years running, Shirley Temple, was only six....
(Right) Future President Ronald Reagan, then just a local Des Moines radio sportscaster, congratulates winning driver Gus Shrader at the 1938 Iowa State Fair Race.

Olympic ice skater/actress Sonja Henie is all smiles in a 1936 Cord Sportsman, and why not? This model 810 was a handsome car indeed, but it was also said to lack power, so the following year a model 812 was supercharged and had little trouble topping 110 mph.

(Above) 1933 Packard Super Eight Coupe Roadster Collection of Bob and Jo Zardin. (Top right and right) 1934 Packard Super Eight

The ever popular Jimmy Stewart and his mother standing beside his princely 1937 Packard 6.

The ultra-rare Rockne two-seater (circa 1931) was named after Notre Dame immortal Knute Rockne. The company, however, was quite mortal and lasted but three years.

sneered upon by sports car purists who preferred Bugattis and Alfa Romeos, this Supercharged 1936 Auburn Speedster (left) was, however, a favorite of Errol Flynn, who enjoyed its ability to exceed 100 mph (guaranteed). In addition to superb styling, the Speedster also had a compartment just for golf clubs on the right side with its own locked door.
The 1934 De Soto and Chrysler Airflow (right) was a technological breakthrough in more ways than just aerodynamically.

Fast, fuel-efficient, comfortable, and safety conscious, the public hated how it looked and bought few.
The 1938 Packard Twelve Touring Sedan (Collection of Harris Laskey) (bottom left)
In the 1937 Buick Century (bottom right), visibility clearly took a backseat to styling.

(Above and right) The 1938 Lincoln Zephyr Convertible Coupe from the collection of Mike Ludwig—with styling such as the burled wood interior and elegant exterior design, this car elicits covetous admiration from collectors and pedestrians alike.

(Left) In 1933, only five Pierce Silver Arrows were built. Years ahead of its time in body design, the Silver Arrow boasted a 175-hp engine that topped out at an incredible 115 mph. With a price tag of $10,000 in the heart of the Great Depression, it's no wonder only five were made.

Part Two

Social Mobility

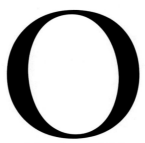

CHAPTER 5

The War Machine

One of the most popular attractions at the 1939 World's Fair in New York was General Motors' Futurama. Each day thousands of people waited in long, serpentine lines outside a huge, white pavilion—just to get a glimpse of GM's vision of American life in the 1960s. And what a vision it was! Magnificent skyscrapers rising out of the urban landscape; cities connected by neatly groomed, multi-lane expressways; traffic humming along smoothly at 100 miles per hour; peaceful commuters and travelers snug and content within their sleek, climate-controlled cars, each with a price tag of approximately $200.

As depicted by industrial designer Norman Bel Geddes, the United States in the 1960s would be a land in which the

Aerial view of the World's Fair in New York, 1939, with an artist's model of the spectacular GM exhibit (inset), which gave visitors a glimpse of the future.

Henry Ford, who had resisted the UAW in 1941 and then settled on what seemed to be very generous terms once it became clear to him that there was no other alternative, was not anxious to see his company devote all of its production to war material. He's a very erratic person at this point in time. It's not clear to me that he was stable as a personality at this point. . . .

I think he was for moral reasons as much as for economic reasons very unsure about World War Two. Very unsure about committing his company and, therefore, himself because it was his name to World War Two.

Now we could also add that Henry Ford had been honored by Nazi Germany. That Henry Ford's own anti-Semitism which he had publicly renounced in the 1920s might still have been an influence in his thinking about America's relationship to Germany at war in Europe.

Ron Edsforth
Historian

automobile would solve virtually every urban problem. Absent from the exhibit were any signs of traffic jams, accidents, carjackers, or smog. It was an undeniably attractive, if hopelessly naive, portrayal. And to a consumer society emerging from the throes of the most prolonged period of economic hardship in the country's history, it was a vision worth embracing.

By 1941, anything seemed possible for the automobile industry. At the dawn of a new decade, the Great Depression was finally loosening its grip on the country. As part of Roosevelt's New Deal, thousands of miles of paved road had been added. Labor disputes that had ravaged the Big Three had been settled; assembly lines were rolling again. And, most important of all, consumer confidence was rising; people wanted cars, and Detroit was eager to meet their needs.

There was, however, one very large problem: the specter of war.

On September 1, 1939, Adolf Hitler had ordered German troops to invade Poland, thus dragging the world inexorably toward war. Over the next two years the U.S. watched nervously as the conflict in Europe and Asia escalated. In late 1940 President Roosevelt urged the country to prepare for the possibility of direct involvement in the war. The U.S., he said, "must be the great arsenal of democracy."

At the time, the United States was hardly a military superpower; in fact, the U.S. Army was only the 19th largest in the world. From a technological standpoint, however, the U.S. was highly advanced. If the country's manufacturing prowess—most clearly visible in Detroit—could be applied toward the prospective war effort, then surely a formidable fighting machine could be constructed. And yet, there was at first a reluctance on the part of the automobile manufacturers to support

this transition.

"When war breaks out in Europe in 1939, the industry is rebounding from what's often called the Roosevelt Recession of 1937–38," says Ron Edsforth. "And it was making good profits, and looking forward to producing more cars for the domestic marketplace, and not seeing the United States get directly involved in the war. Some of the people associated with General Motors were in fact involved in funding the America First movement, which was calling for the United States to stay out of this second major war in Europe in a generation. So, on the whole, the industry was not anxious to see a loss

of profits due to a shift to war production."

War in Europe, prior to U.S. involvement, looked less like the economic boost it would become than a threat to the country's recovery. So, as long as the country was at peace—even if that peace was tenuous—industry leaders did not want to divert their attention away from the American consumer. In an attempt to encourage greater peacetime involvement on the part of the auto manufacturers, Roosevelt persuaded General Motors President William Knudsen to become co-director (along with Sidney Hillman, president of the Amalgamated Clothing Workers) of the Office of Production Management, which would oversee industrial preparation for the war.

Unfortunately, the OPM had precious little clout; participation in the buildup for war remained a voluntary act, and the automobile industry continued to drag its feet, even as other industries warmed to the idea.

Meanwhile, the UAW was squarely behind the war effort. Shortly after Germany invaded Poland,

William Knudsen and Henry Ford in better times, before Knudsen defected to GM. Knudsen's selection to direct Detroit's war effort from Washington, D.C., further annoyed Ford, a pacifist who admired Germany, distrusted Washington, and despised his former employee.

Walter Reuther had sent a proposal to Washington in which he outlined a plan to convert the auto industry to aircraft production; it was Reuther's contention that Detroit could manufacture as many as 50,000 planes in a single year. Industry executives at the time generally viewed Reuther's plan as thoroughly misguided. It also set the stage

for a public relations struggle between labor and management. Once the U.S. entered World War II, each wanted to be recognized as being the most patriotic.

"Walter Reuther is certainly perceived by supporters of the Roosevelt Administration as someone who is much more anxious to get involved in supporting war production and preparedness and then preparation for actually sending American troops abroad than the auto company executives," says Ron Edsforth. "But one of the things that would happen during the war is that this image of the auto industry as reluctant would dissipate, would disappear."

On December 7, 1941, the Japanese attack on Pearl Harbor finally pulled the United States into the war. Really, though, the country was not yet *ready* for war. Against long odds, the OPM had managed to set the stage for wartime production, but virtually nothing had been manufactured. So it was something of a miracle that the U.S. was able to shift all of its manufacturing capabilities toward military production in such a short period of time.

Of course, public and political pressure left no other option. The isolationist movement of the late 1930s was dead; the war was on. Assembly line workers traded overalls for uniforms (in many cases, their places on the line were temporarily filled by wives and girlfriends left behind). Some industry executives—Knudsen being the most visible—became involved in war agencies in Washington; others contributed through their work in Detroit, which bordered on the spectacular. Many historians now regard the production of war materials in the United States as the decisive factor in determining the outcome of World War II. And the automobile industry played a leading role in that production, turning out more than 5.9 million weapons, 2.8 million tanks and trucks, and 27,000 fully assembled aircraft. These materials were manufactured not only for U.S. soldiers, but for all of the allied forces.

"On the eve of World War II, what the industry did is not simply begin to expand production," says Harley Shaiken. "It was a human effort in terms of manufacturing that didn't simply produce

December 7, 1941—Pearl Harbor, Hawaii

When my brother Walter put forward to the President of the United States and to the congress his proposal for building 500 airplanes a day in the automobile industry, the industry guffawed and said, 'Oh, that's nonsense.' And, of course, history proved that Walter was correct—by war's end corporate leaders boasted that they had converted well over 85% of their then existing capacity for military production.

So the trade union by vigorously pushing for rapid conversion not only helped our members—who were thrown out of work when the government orders cut off the use of steel for peace time products —we also helped the nation enormously by pushing the war effort into fast forward. And I think Americans at large do not understand the crucial role which the American labor movement played in early mobilization for the war against Hitler.

Victor Reuther
UAW leader

These M-5 light tanks rolled off General Motors' assembly line in South Gate, CA on April 20, 1943. The result of an extensive sub-contracting system among Los Angeles manufacturers, only the motive power and transmission units were shipped to the South Gate plant from outside the state.

a bit more or even a lot more; it totally redefined what people could do in an amazingly short period of time. To call it an industrial miracle would not overstate the case. When Detroit was referred to extensively as the Arsenal of Democracy, it meant just that. It was a productive capability that went beyond what anyone could have imagined a decade before. And it didn't simply happen after a burst of productive activity. It happened after the industry was rusting and coming unstuck in the 1930s. So you had a production facility that was literally grasping and crawling along, satisfied simply to survive, overnight becoming the Arsenal of Democracy. And that redefined what was possible."

While patriotism surely played a part in Detroit's massive contribution to the war effort, so too did practicality. The war, once fully joined, was good business for the automobile industry. The United States government, to ensure full partici-

heartache and death and destruction, it was World War II (and the industrial mobilization it prompted) that lifted the U.S., once and for all, out of the Great Depression.

General Motors produced its last automobile, a Chevrolet, on January 30, 1942. Eleven days later the last Ford rolled off the assembly line. Automobile production came to a complete halt as the government sought to conserve steel and other materials. The few cars produced in 1942 were not put on the market; rather, they were reserved primarily for government officials and military personnel.

By the end of February, virtually every automotive plant in the country was in the process of being retooled for the production of military equipment. The transition was impressive, if not always smooth. Chrysler built a new factory—featuring an assembly line one-third of a mile long—specifically for the production of Sherman tanks. General Motors produced anti-aircraft weapons and also used V-8 engines and automatic transmissions to make M-5 tanks. Never before had the concept of mass production been so effectively applied to a military operation. Tasks that in other countries had typically taken days—even weeks—could now be achieved in a matter of hours. It was nothing less than a technological wonder, and it allowed the U.S. to quickly outfit the 13 million men and women who joined the armed services during World War II.

pation on the part of the nation's industrial organizations, established a system through which manufacturers would be guaranteed profits regardless of the cost of production. On that basis, the automobile industry—and all other industries— were more than happy to cooperate.

Moreover, they were handsomely rewarded by a massive wartime construction program. Shortly after the U.S. entered the war, the federal government announced that it would spend $11 billion to build manufacturing plants dedicated exclusively to the production of defense materials. After the war, the government promised, the plants would be sold back to private industry at a substantial discount.

For the automobile manufacturers (and their employees and shareholders), it was an enormously attractive deal: a chance to contribute to the war effort, make a profit, and significantly increase post war production capability. Ironically, for all its

Perhaps the most impressive example of Detroit's ingenuity could be seen in Ford's massive Willow Run plant, which produced B-24 Liberator bombers. Before the U.S. entered the war, Henry Ford had declared rather cavalierly that his company could produce one thousand planes per day—provided there was no interference from labor unions or the federal government. Willow Run never approached those numbers, but eventually it did prove to be a triumph of mass production. Along the way, though, the project suffered its share of setbacks.

Like most Big Three executives, Henry Ford was not anxious to see his company devote all its production to war material. But his trepidation was greater than most other people's. For one thing, he respected Germany; and the feeling was mutual. At the age of 75, in fact, Ford had received from Hitler emissaries the Supreme Order of the German Eagle. This had less to do with any philosophical bond than an admiration for Ford's record of technological achievement. In truth, Henry Ford was vehemently anti-war; he was a pacifist, just as he had been during World War I, and so he had difficulty embracing the American war effort under any circumstances. Moreover, he was perturbed by the selection of William Knudsen—a former Ford employee who had defected to GM—as the man who would direct Detroit's war effort from Washington.

Ground was broken for the Willow Run plant in April of 1941, on a vast chunk of land near Ypsilanti, Michigan. Originally, Ford was asked only to build subassemblies for Consolidated Aircraft, but Charles Sorensen, who headed the project, had pushed for a deal that would allow Ford to construct the entire B-24. The contract included $200 million for the construction of a new factory—the largest in the world. In exchange, Sorensen said, Ford would manufacture more than 500 planes per month, a figure ten times greater than Consolidated's capability. This would be accomplished, of course, through the miracle of mass production. Just like a car, the B-24 Liberator bomber would be broken down into components and dragged along an assembly line.

Henry Ford, whose behavior was becoming increasingly unpredictable, tried to block the construction of the Willow Run plant, even after granting Sorensen the authority to close the deal.

Sorensen and Edsel Ford eventually gave the project final approval despite Henry's protestations.

"In some ways, Willow Run is one of the marvels of the industrial world," notes Ron Edsforth. "Yet it's something that Henry Ford himself was never very comfortable with; that the Ford Motor Company itself really never wanted. And so it would dispose of it at the end of the war."

View of the manufacturing section of the Ford Willow Run plant, which stretches over half a mile.

The car factories which had been built in the 1930s were the major landmarks of America's might. These were huge things. And they were talked about in song and in art and in popular culture. These were really extraordinary monuments, unknown before in the history of the world and certainly a characteristic of the American way of life. So all of those national assets were devoted to the defense of the country during the war.

What's interesting though is that even though they were converted to a different use, they were still in their own way preparing for the future, because the demands of the war were for new types of engines, new types of metals that would withstand higher temperatures, new types of technology like radar, plastics, glass, types of materials which could help the war effort obviously. Make strong, faster, more powerful planes, ships, whatever.

The car companies did give themselves to the defense effort of the nation. But it was also an opportunity for them to explore new materials, to push the technology as far as it could. All of these things were to have their fruit also in a consumer sense after the war ended.

Alan Hess
Historian

For quite some time, Willow Run was far less than the technological showcase Sorensen had predicted. The project suffered from an assortment of problems: squabbling between Henry Ford, Edsel Ford, Sorensen, and Harry Bennett; governmental interference; and the loss of thousands of workers to the military draft. The first Liberator was not produced until September of 1942, the same month in which President Roosevelt expressed his concern by personally visiting the plant. By the end of 1942, only 56 B-24s had been manufactured at Willow Run, which had now been saddled with the derisive moniker, "Willit Run?"

Army Air Force officials were still asking that question in early 1943 and actually gave serious consideration to requesting that control of the

Willow Run plant be turned over to the federal government. J.H. Kindelberger, president of North American Aviation (an organization that obviously had no desire to see the automobile industry infringe on its territory), chastised Detroit for its perceived arrogance. "You cannot expect blacksmiths to learn how to make watches overnight," he said.

NO TIME TO LET LOOSE !

It's a Fight to a Finish!

The incredible contribution by Detroit to the war effort was embodied—among many things—by the B-24 Liberator bomber, shown here in action. After getting some of the kinks out, the Ford Willow Run plant produced a bomber every 63 minutes, for a total production of 8,500. As the war-time poster shown above exemplifies, Americans—like Detroit factories—were asked to give their best, and the total effort surpassed expectation.

Just as it seemed that Sorensen was going to be forced to admit defeat, however, "Willit Run?" became Willow Run, with B-24 Liberator bombers streaming out the door on a regular basis. The project had been far more daunting than Sorensen had anticipated, but eventually it proved worthwhile. Ford produced 190 bombers in June of 1943; by December, the monthly figure was 365; by the middle of 1944, Willow Run was turning out an average of one B-24 bomber every 63 minutes, a rate that allowed the price of the planes to be cut nearly in half.

"Willow Run looked like a city with a roof on it," remembers Ester Earthlene, one of the many thousands of women who joined the work force during the war. "You just walked in and you looked up and you didn't see any sky. But it was huge, and there were large trucks driving around, and cars driving around. It was just fantastic. Some of the pictures I've seen of us that were taken, we looked like little creatures crawling around, walking around. It was so big, and there were so many of us. And we were always working

WILLYS PRODUCTION MODEL
VIEW FROM RIGHT FRONT SIDE

RT-176   W.O.ENG.NO. 1374   10-9-43

The familiar Willys-Overland Jeep was a war baby. The Jeep also had a baby—today's sports utility vehicles. Where did the name "Jeep" originate? One theory: They were originally called G.P.s for General Purpose until Gee Pee became Jeep.

at top speed. But after the first few planes, you know, everyone had experience, and it was a rhythmic type of a thing. You had to do a job and so many minutes to do it in. And you did it. I guess you'd say it was a really good assembly line."

By the end of the war, Willow Run's 43,000 workers had produced more than 8,500 bombers; in its final months, the plant's output exceeded even Sorensen's lofty expectations. There was to be no celebration on his part, however, for he was by then already a victim of Harry Bennett's vengeful and covetous nature. Sorensen left Ford before the end of the war and later served for a short time as president of Willys-Overland.

The work accomplished at Willow Run, while

perhaps more spectacular than at some other plants, was reflective of Detroit's tremendous contribution to the war effort. The military equipment produced by the automobile industry cost approximately $29 billion, a figure that represents one-fifth of the war materials produced in the United States. Obviously this could not have occurred without massive contributions from both labor and management, whose generally antagonistic relationship softened somewhat as World War II escalated; to some degree, it seemed, each side was swept up in the rising tide of patriotism.

"Willow Run was just fascinating," recalls Ester Earthlene. "And it was well-managed and the foremen were nice. It wasn't until after Willow

Run that I had experience with bad foremen.

"During the war it was kind of like a high. It was like everybody's adrenaline was rolling, going top speed because we had a job to do—and it was important. And there were always people around. They had three different housing projects at Willow Run: one for the singles, one for married couples, and one for families. And every person who owned a house had a rooming house or apartment house. So everything was full. Everything was going three shifts, 24 hours a day. You could go to the movies 24 hours a day. You could go to the post office. You could go to the cafeteria or laundry. It was tiring, but it was exciting. It's a feeling that…no one can really describe how it was."

Ford also played a major role in the production of another famous war machine—one that would, in fact, later become a cultural icon: the jeep. The U.S. Army began soliciting offers for a simple, versatile vehicle in 1939. The original design was submitted by the American Bantam Car Company, a tiny, and not terribly profitable, manufacturer of small cars. The army loved Bantam's initial design; however, by the time it was prepared to accept bids, Bantam was no longer the only player in the game. Willys-Overland had also jumped into the fray—with a vehicle that was every inch the equal of Bantam's. The Willys jeep was similar in basic design, and featured four-wheel drive, masked fender-mount con-

It was only during the war that all the women started to go to work in the factories. That's when I went back to work—after I got married and had children —in a defense plant. And that's when I got my first car and when women all over the country began to say, 'Hey, here I am.'

I mean you could get up and if you wanted to do something you could just go out in your car and go. You didn't have to depend on your husband or anybody else to drive or take you someplace.

Job, car, independence. To me it meant everything. It meant freedom.

Jo Newswanger
Witness

voy nightlights, and a rifle rack under the windshield.

Since Willys submitted a lower bid—and had far superior production capabilities—it received the contract. In the next five years, with a substantial amount of assistance from Ford, some 660,000 jeeps poured off the assembly lines. The tough little open-air jeep quickly became a symbol of American spirit and resiliency; it could, and did, go anywhere. Award-winning cartoonist Bill Mauldin immortalized the jeep in a famous cartoon featuring a weeping soldier firing a bullet into his broken-down jeep—as if the vehicle were an injured horse that had to be put out of its misery.

The source of the vehicle's name, incidentally, has been disputed for decades. The most popular, and likely, explanation is that the army requested a "general purpose" vehicle. General purpose became G.P., which in turn became …"jeep."

No matter. A jeep by any other name would still sell as swiftly. The jeep of the 1940s was the grandfather of the sport utility vehicle, which by 1996 had claimed a healthy share of the new-car market in the United States.

"The jeep iconography is all about war and heroes," says Laurel Cutler, a former vice president of Chrysler who now works in New York as a marketing executive specializing in consumerism. "And an idealistic war, which was World War II.

The jeep had all of the romance of that great and successful war to it."

Of course, in Detroit, as in Europe and the Pacific, the war was not all about romance. Certainly the automobile industry's ability to transform itself into Roosevelt's Arsenal of Democracy was an enormous achievement. And it's hard not to be somewhat sentimental about the valiant role played by women and minorities, a large percentage of whom had previously had little access to the comparatively high-paying jobs in Detroit (with abundant overtime opportunities).

At the same time, there was an ugly side to the technological explosion created by the war. As the migration of African Americans from the rural south to the industrial north reached its peak in the mid-1940s, racial tension mounted. In 1943, 34 people in Detroit died in race riots that began when a group of white workers, fearing they might lose their jobs, pulled blacks from streetcars and beat them to death. But the violence could not halt progress. A decade earlier, black workers fortunate enough to secure positions in the overwhelmingly white automobile industry usually were assigned to the foundry, where they performed the most dangerous and difficult jobs in the plant. By the time the war ended, though, the face of the American work force had changed forever. Integration had become a fact of life on the assembly line. And if there was something less than overt affection between the races, there was, at least, a sense of solidarity. They were workers, union men...*brothers.*

"That's not to say that we have not had our differences, racial differences, within the union movement," says former Detroit mayor Coleman Young, who worked for many years in the auto industry. "But as contrasted with the racial attitudes of a society beyond the union, I think there's no question that the union stands out as one of the high points of interracial unity within our society."

As for the consumer, his love affair with the car was severely tested during World War II. This relationship had evolved over a period of decades, and certain parameters had been established. The

American automobile owner had come to believe that it was his inalienable right to drive as far and as fast and as often as he liked. Now, though, the rules had been changed. Life had changed.

That there were no new cars available was only part of the problem. Most motorists could accept with a patriotic nod the decision to produce tanks and B-24 bombers instead of automobiles; they would simply make do with their old vehicles, even if they were beginning to deteriorate. Harder to swallow were the shortages of other resources that

(Above) A group of migratory workers from Florida in the early 1940s on their way to look for opportunity in the north, in this case New Jersey for prospects in agriculture. But the war created better opportunities for minorities. At the Packard factory in 1948 (right), an African-American foreman supervises African-American assembly line workers during the company's most successful year since the heyday of 1927.

contributed to the well-being of the family car, and which had previously been taken for granted.

Rubber, for example, became extremely scarce, thanks largely to Japanese dominance in the Far East. The U.S. had stockpiled a year's supply of before prior to its involvement in the war, but virtually all of it was targeted for use by the military; the few factories that made synthetic rubber also found the military to be their primary customer. So dire was the situation that the federal government was forced to impose severe restrictions on the use of rubber. As a result, most families found themselves patching and repatching old tires in an effort to keep their cars on the road. For regardless of the condition of an automobile, it was all but useless without tires. And new tires could be purchased only with ration stamps from the Office of Price Administration—stamps that were almost impossible for civilians to obtain.

Similarly, by the middle of 1942, gasoline rationing had become standard practice in the Northeastern United States; not because the supply had been exhausted or cut off, but because submarine attacks in the Gulf of Mexico and along the Atlantic seaboard had destroyed much of the tanker fleet that delivered the fuel. With gasoline and rubber in such short supply, and with so many people reliant upon their cars to get to work (in many cases their jobs were directly related to the war effort), the country was facing a crisis. The

government responded by establishing a national speed limit of 40 miles per hour (later reduced to 35 mph) in the hope of minimizing wear and tear on tires. Within six months, though, it was apparent that more drastic measures were needed. The only solution was to find a way to limit the use of automobiles. So, on December 1, 1942, a national policy of gas rationing—designed to discourage unnecessary driving—went into effect.

Each automobile owner was required to place a sticker bearing the letter A, B, C or X on his windshield. The number of gasoline coupons he could purchase was determined by his place in the OPA pecking order. An A sticker entitled the driver to four gallons of gasoline per week; more went to the holder of a B sticker (typically reserved for workers directly involved in the war effort, travelling in car pools); and more still to the doctors and corporate executives who received C stickers. Unlimited allotment was reserved for those fortunate few (congressmen, senators, high-ranking government officials) whose windshields were emblazoned with the letter X.

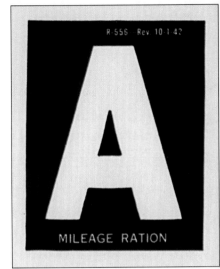

"You prized your coupons for gasoline like you wouldn't believe it," remembers Alvalee Arnold, who lived and worked in Texas during the war. "And you didn't use your gas for anything ordinary. If you could walk, you walked. And you used your gas for special trips, vacations or shopping trip. Things that were important. But you were very selective. I remember our friends gave us A coupons for gas so we could go down to New Orleans on our honeymoon. That was quite a gift."

Despite abuses of the system (somehow, only half the cars in the nation wound up with A stickers; and, predictably, a thriving black market for all rationed supplies—especially gasoline—emerged during the war), gas rationing succeeded in curtailing automobile use by more than 40 percent. Nevertheless, time and circumstance had taken their toll on the American automobile. By the time World War II came to an end, more than 4,000 cars were being scrapped each day; and there were no new cars to fill the void. Demand for automobiles had never been greater, but Detroit was stuck in neutral.

CHAPTER 6

The Post-War Boom

In the final months of World War II, the automobile industry began pumping more money into advertising. There were two messages for the American consumer: First, that automakers were fulfilling their patriotic duty by supporting the war effort; second, that war technology would be used to manufacture better consumer products as soon as the war ended. Meanwhile, behind the scenes, designers and engineers were letting their imaginations run wild. Using the streamlined cars of the 1930s as a starting point and incorporating dramatic war imagery, they began to conceive the first postwar automobiles. When the fighting finally came to an end, a new attitude swept across America. The bloodiest war in history was over, and the United States had emerged as the world's dominant military and economic power. Advertising quite

The infamous gap-toothed grin of the powerful Buick Roadmaster and its "Big Eight" engine (circa 1949) greeted many a driver in his rear view mirror before passing him on the left.

The 1946 Detroit Automotive Golden Jubilee Motor City Cavalcade was a celebration of the resumption of consumer car manufacturing. Above, the S.S. Oldsmobile floats past the reviewing stand. The Jubilee held a Pioneers Tribute, after which old friends gathered to talk about old times. At left, Henry Ford shares a smile with Barney Oldfield, the legendary race car driver of the Ford 999 that broke the 1904 world land speed record. Watching on the left is car maker Charles Nash, and on the right, George Romney, who in ten years would form AMC from the rubble of Nash-Hudson.

naturally reflected that status. One General Motors commercial, for example, depicted a Buick triumphantly rising from the ashes of war.

It was a potent image. Soldiers returning home, after all, wanted nothing more than to get on with their lives. They wanted to start families. They wanted to purchase new homes and new cars. They wanted all of the things that had seemed impossible before World War II, when the country was suffocating under the weight of the Great Depression. Now, there was a sense that the world had changed, that America as depicted in the 1939 Futurama exhibit was soon to become a reality. Consumer confidence was soaring.

"The expectation after World War II was that the good life was finally here," says author and historian Alan Hess. "Something better than the 1930s had provided. Certainly something better than the war had offered. And so when consumers saw it being offered to them, in advertisements, on supermarket shelves, in department stores, in car dealerships, they were ready and willing and eager to support it. And at that time they had the money to do so."

Immediately after the war, Detroit began the laborious process of retooling for automobile production. In the beginning, the car companies simply offered their old, prewar models. Nothing fancy. Nothing dramatic. It would be two more years before completely redesigned products were introduced. Motorists could not have cared less. If these were old designs, they were nonetheless *new* cars, and they were snatched up in short order.

Automobile industry executives expected this, of course. Not since the early days of the Model T had demand for new cars been so great. Automobile production

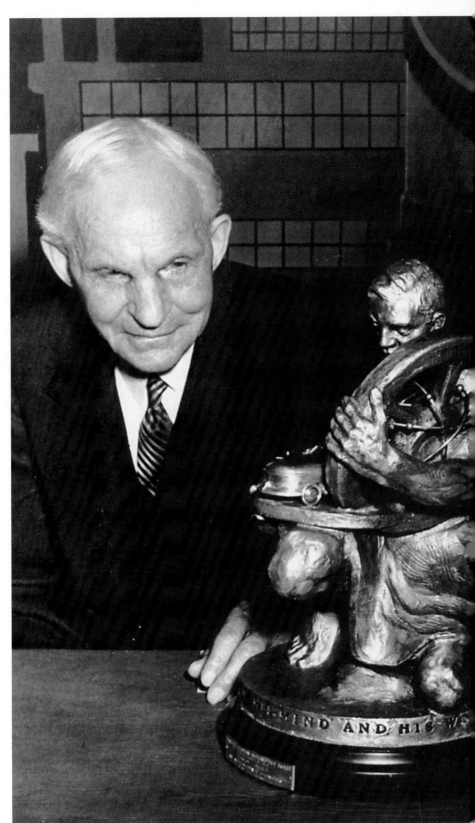

Henry Ford gazes upon the Clifton Award bestowed upon him at the 1946 Golden Jubilee Tribute for his pioneering work on behalf of the automobile industry.

In a vain attempt to compete with the Big Three, Joseph W. Frazer (right) joined forces with Henry Kaiser in 1947. The Kaiser's two-door sedan was a fine car and initially sold well in 1947, but it had less power and cost more than the Big Three's products, so production ceased in 1951.

had slipped from 3.2 million in 1941 to 223,000 in 1942; over the next three years production had been virtually non-existent. During World War II, automobile registration fell by four million as cars either died of old age or were put on blocks while their owners went off to fight. Add to this the fact that many consumers had been either unable or unwilling to buy a new car during the Great Depression, and you have an automobile drought that lasted nearly 16 years. By the end of 1945, an estimated half of the 26 million automobiles registered in the United States had been purchased at least a decade earlier.

Americans found almost everything to be in short supply during the war, but nothing seemed quite so vital as the automobile. With Germany's collapse in 1945, the federal government authorized the production of 200,000 passenger cars; when the war in the Pacific ended, production limits

were lifted, and Detroit shifted as quickly as possible into high gear.

At the same time, consumers began lining up at automobile showrooms. Dealers discovered that they could not keep pace with demand, which naturally triggered concern that prices would skyrocket. As a preemptive measure, the Office of Price Administration mandated that new cars sold in 1945 must be sold at 1942 prices. While this was a noble gesture, it was not a panacea. For one thing, unscrupulous car dealers often sidestepped the OPA rules by driving new cars once or twice around the block and then putting them on the market as "used"—sometimes for several hundred dollars more than the OPA limit for new cars.

Automobile manufacturers also ran into difficulty. Technical problems stemming from the retooling process led to delays in production; so, too, did labor problems. Although wages during the war had remained steady, overtime pay had allowed workers to make substantial gains. The UAW, well aware of the potential for inflation, fought to keep overall income consistent with wartime levels. Management, naturally, rejected this notion. As a result, the industry endured several strikes—the longest being a 119-day walkout at General Motors in the winter of 1946.

Soon, however, the assembly lines were moving at full speed. The 1947 Studebaker—sleek, streamlined...*new!*— was the first postwar-designed car to appear on showroom floors. The Big Three did not introduce new models until late 1948, but by then pent-up demand had resulted in a huge backlog of orders—despite the termination of OPA price limits. At one point General Motors had outstanding orders for five million cars. Never had there been such a seller's market.

"After the war the industry discovers that it has a huge marketplace full of consumers who will buy almost anything they produce," says Ron Edsforth. "And this means that all the industries that supply the auto industry will boom along with it. This rapidly expands the automobile-based society. It establishes the ability to extend mass consumerism beyond the sort of wall it had run up against in the late 1920s, and creates the greatest prosperity in American history. Many industries are participating and contributing to the economic boom. But because the automobile industry has the largest economic impact, the greatest multiplier effect, I think it's undeniable that its role is crucial."

General Motors and Chrysler weathered the war years reasonably well, largely because of consistent leadership in their executive offices. William Knudsen (who died in 1948 after leading Detroit's war

The postwar prosperity manifested itself in many ways. (Above) The first of what would become many "Drive-In" markets. (Below) Customers examine the merchandise at a Lancaster, Ohio, used car lot in 1938.

effort) was succeeded by Charles E. Wilson at General Motors, where Alfred P. Sloan's system of team management and flexibility served the company well in periods of potentially jarring transition. In fact, General Motors benefited enormously from the war. Already the largest and most profitable company in the industry when the war began, GM increased its productive capacity by as much as $1 billion through government-subsidized wartime construction. By the end of the war, GM was in a position to claim a 50 percent share of the market.

At Chrysler, K.T. Keller remained in the president's office throughout the war and effectively guided the company until his retirement in 1950.

Even the independents—Studebaker, Nash, Packard, Hudson, and Willys-Overland—found the war years to be profitable, since they too were

(Above) General Motors became the most powerful corporation in the world under the guidance of Alfred P. Sloan Jr., shown here in 1946. (Below) Traffic begins to mount on California's Arroyo Parkway also known as the Pasadena Freeway.

involved in military production. Their confidence and ledgers bolstered, the independents began the postwar era with grand aspirations, optimistic that the market was now healthy enough to accommodate smaller manufacturers. And for a while, at least, it seemed they were right; the independents were the first to resume full production of passenger vehicles, and that efficiency allowed them to capture a 15 percent share of the passenger-car market.

Of the Big Three, Ford emerged from World War II with the most scars. Despite receiving billions of dollars in military contracts, the company was unable to turn a profit. Beset by mismanagement and an ongoing internal power struggle, Ford lost as much as $10 million a month during the war. The problems began escalating in May of 1943, when Edsel Ford succumbed to stomach cancer, leaving no clear line of succession to the Ford throne. Henry Ford, 80 years old and weakened both physically and mentally by two strokes, assumed the presidency. In effect, he was nothing more than a figurehead; in the shadows, preparing to take over, was Harry Bennett.

Ford stockholders, of course, were concerned about the future of their company; so, too, was the U.S. government, which desperately needed Ford to maintain a high level of productivity in support of the war effort. So, in that same year, Henry Ford's grandson, Henry II, was discharged from the U.S. Navy and allowed to return home, in the hope that he could rescue the sagging Ford Motor Company.

Young Henry found the firm in disarray. Morale was low. Accountants stacked bills in piles and measured them with rulers to estimate costs.

Like grandfather, like grandson—Henry Ford II poses beside his grandfather, Henry, and grandmother, Clara, on the historic quadricycle shortly after Henry II's hostile takeover of the company from Harry Bennett.

"Hank the Deuce" was a smart and thoughtful man, much like his father, but stronger of will. He spent several weeks quietly digesting Edsel's private notes before taking any action. Then he took the first step: getting his grandfather to retire. It wasn't easy. In addition to dealing with Harry Bennett (so fearful were young Henry and his assistants that they often carried pistols to the office), Henry II had to enlist the aid of his mother and grandmother in the battle against the elder Ford. In the end, Henry Ford consented to retire only after Edsel's widow, Eleanor, threatened to sell all of the Ford stock she had inherited from her husband—41 percent of the company.

On September 21, 1945, Henry Ford II was elected president of the Ford Motor Company. Harry Bennett was fired that very day; before leaving he provoked an armed confrontation (guns were drawn, but no shots fired) with John S. Bugas, a former Detroit FBI chief who had become one of Ford's top aides, and set a small fire in his office, using his private papers as fuel.

With the war ended, Henry II hired a group of brilliant young executives from the Harvard Business School—nicknamed the "Whiz Kids"—to usher in a new era. Among the group was Robert S. McNamara, who became president of Ford and, during the Vietnam War, U.S. Secretary of Defense. For the crucial position of executive vice president, Henry II turned to Ernest R. Breech, a General Motors alumnus who had become head of Bendix Aviation. In less than two years time, a completely new regime was established and Ford's fortunes were beginning to turn.

As for Henry Ford, a complex man who gave

1949

Lincoln
has a new idea

THAT ADDS TO THE ZEST OF FINE-CAR DRIVING!

The Lincolns' new individual front-wheel suspension floats you over the roughest roads.

The new 1949 Lincoln and Lincoln Cosmopolitan are keyed to a new idea: to give you truly fine cars...luxurious and powerful...yet *easy* to handle ...*easy* to drive...*easy* on you!

You sense the Lincoln Idea the instant you see the exciting new lines of these great new cars. Massive and powerful-looking, low and buoyant... they have a *look* of confident, easy fleetness.

You meet the Lincoln Idea in the completely new power plant. Eight-cylinder, V-type, 152-horse-power strong, it has been built with a new flexibility that lets you maneuver *easily* in traffic, sure of its quick, ready response.

On the road, the balanced strength of Lincoln's extra-rigid chassis, plus new spring suspension give a new, steady roadability. You'll like the in-

stant response of Lincoln's great new brakes.

Big picture windows and wide windshields let you see more...and more *easily*. Interiors are superb in their beauty and luxury.

This year your fine-car decision should be *easy! So Look Into Lincoln...the fine car that makes to-day's hard driving conditions easy on you!*
LINCOLN-MERCURY DIVISION OF FORD MOTOR COMPANY

White side-wall tires, road lamps and rear wheel shields (on the Lincoln) are optional

The one-piece curved picture windshield in the Lincoln Cosmopolitan gives you greater visibility...a typical example of the Lincoln Idea of easier-on-you driving.

Power and economy star in the Lincolns' new 152-horsepower engine. Shown, the Lincoln.

THE LINCOLN IDEA IS YOURS TO ENJOY IN **THE LINCOLN** AND **THE LINCOLN COSMOPOLITAN.** THESE TWO COMPLETELY NEW 1949 CARS ARE IN TWO SEPARATE PRICE RANGES AND A CHOICE OF MAGNIFICENT BODY STYLES.

birth to one of the most successful corporations in history, he drifted into senility and died quietly in 1947.

"Henry Ford was very eccentric in many ways," observes Harley Shaiken. "But the difference between being eccentric and being a genius is a billion-dollar-a-year industry. Henry Ford's ability to have exceptional and path-breaking productivity made many of his eccentric ideas—I mean, he made soy beans in the River Rouge plant—all of a sudden not simply acceptable but studied at length. Henry Ford had a vision of what it meant to be an American. But he also had a very dark side."

The first completely redesigned postwar car produced by one of the Big Three was the 1949 Ford, unveiled in June of 1948 at the Waldorf-Astoria Hotel in New York. Before that, Ford, like Chrysler and General Motors, had simply made slight changes to its 1942 models and fed them to a ravenous public. The '49 Ford was different. Aside from its reliable V-8 engine, nothing about the car seemed familiar. It was longer, sleeker. It was...*stylish*.

The car had gone from drawing board to showrooms in just 18 months time, at a cost of nearly $120 million. The tight production schedule inevitably led to glitches and defects, and customers routinely returned the car to dealers for mechanical adjustments. No one really complained, though. The '49 Ford looked great. Customers were perfectly willing to accept a few problems—so long as they were quickly repaired; dealers could scarcely keep up with demand. At Ford headquarters, of course, there was a collective sigh of relief. After a slump that had lasted more than 15 years, business was booming. New car sales in 1949 were more than double what they had been the previous year. In 1950 Ford sur-

passed the one million mark in annual sales for the first time since the glory days of the Model T, and moved back into second place among the Big Three, behind General Motors but ahead of Chrysler.

Throughout the industry, life had never been better. Automobile showrooms were packed. Motorists took what they could get, rarely bothering to haggle over a sticker price or even the color of a car.

The suave, stylish 1949 Ford was the first truly modern car of the post-war era and would lead an industry wide sales surge that saw new car purchases double over 1948's figures.

"Everybody expected that we'd go from the production of war goods to the production of automobiles almost overnight," remembers Robert Lund, a former General Motors executive. "That wasn't the case. There was a great deal that had to be done in order to get ready to build new automobiles. So initially, of course, immediately following the cessation of the war and the beginning of production, cars were very similar to the cars that had been produced before the war. And then there was the anticipation of a gradual changing of cars and bringing out new models. And when they did come, people got very, very excited about them. As a matter of fact, one of the outstanding things that used to take place was that automobile dealers would be shipped the new cars, ready for the introduction, and they would hide them from the public. There would be this great element of surprise that would take place and all of a sudden on such and such a date, the date selected for the announcement of the new cars, these cars would appear on the showroom floors and people would flock into dealerships just to see the new cars.

"We tried to create an aura of excitement and mystery and anticipation. So we papered all the windows, or we painted the windows. Whatever. We kept the cars out of sight from the general public in anticipation of this day when we'd introduce them. And when the day came, it was like New Year's. People were excited. People brought their children. We had gifts for the kids. We had gifts for the parents. And we just couldn't tell them enough about these brand new cars that were so

beautifully displayed on the showroom floor."

So strong was the new car market that the postwar boom gave rise to several brash, new independent manufacturers. Among the more noteworthy were Preston "P.T." Tucker, a Chicago businessman who created 51 undeniably remarkable automobiles before his company folded and he was indicted on 31 counts of fraud; Powell Crosley, purveyor of a tiny, four-cylinder car that was efficient, but simply too small for a country with big dreams; and California shipbuilder Henry J. Kaiser.

Kaiser teamed up with Joseph W. Frazer, president of the Graham-Paige Motor

Tucker Topics, *the official publication of the Tucker Corporation was sent out in 1948 to all authorized Tucker dealers to assist them in presenting their unique car to the public. Preston Tucker wanted his dealers to feel the same pride in the product that he himself felt so deeply.*

The Tucker had many novel features, like six exhaust pipes, a third headlight that turned with the wheels, and a "bomb shelter" in the back seat. But it also went 0-60 in ten seconds and over 120 mph. Eagerly awaited by a war-deprived public, Preston Tucker was derailed by the Securities and Exchange Commission over fraudulent stock deals.

Company, after World War II, and for a time, the Kaiser-Frazer Corporation became a formidable player in the automotive game. With the help of a $44 million loan, Kaiser-Frazer acquired Ford's old Willow Run plant and began producing automobiles in 1946. Within two years the Kaiser-Frazer line had claimed 5 percent of the domestic passenger car market. But as the Big Three completed the postwar retooling process and began to design new models, the new kids on the block felt the inevitable pinch. By 1953 Kaiser-Frazer had been reborn as the Kaiser Motors Corporation, which owned Willys-Overland. In 1955 the company stopped manufacturing passenger cars and devoted all of its resources to the Jeep and various commercial vehicles.

By the end of the decade, most of the independents would feel the squeeze of the Big Three. In 1954 Nash-Kelvinator merged with Hudson to form the American Motors Corporation; similarly, Studebaker and Packard became the Studebaker-Packard Corporation. But even those consolidations were not sufficient. AMC discontinued the Nash and Hudson in 1957 and concentrated on its low-priced Rambler; the following year Studebaker-Packard faded from the scene.

Meanwhile, at General Motors, the future was *now*. With the 1948 Cadillac came the first subtle signs of an impending revolution—the opening volley in what would come to be known as the Fin Wars of the 1950s.

Actually, the bumps that appeared on the rear fenders of the 1948 Cadillac barely qualified as tail fins—at least by the garish standards set in the 1950s. But they were fins, nonetheless. As for their purpose, well...there wasn't any. The fin performed no useful function. It was purely decorative, although it gave the car an appearance of power and speed—which, of course, was precisely the point. The tail fin was the brainchild of GM styling wizard Harley Earl, who was among the first automobile executives to suggest that war imagery was not only useful in advertising, but on the assembly line.

"The tail fin was just another expression of style, of speed, of flow, of all those things, actually, that

The 1950 Hudson Pacemaker 500 was considered a fine car, but sales dwindled until the company succumbed to the Big Three like countless other independents. Hudson merged with Nash before starting AMC, which was eventually bought out by Chrysler.

The unique styling of this 1951 Buick Le Sabre made it a popular export, eventually finding its way onto the style-conscious streets of Paris, France.

The critically acclaimed 1951 Kaiser two-door sedan was innovative in many respects: the greatest window visibility in the industry, a full length instrument panel crash pad and choices of automatic transmission or overdrive, but it failed to acquire a V-8 engine and Americans rejected it after the first successful year.

have nothing to do with an automobile but have very much to do with fashion," notes Bradford Snell. "And it came into vogue right after the war, when the American soldiers were returning, the flyers were returning. This was when America was caught up with the glamour of fast planes, military planes, aviation. And Sloan was smart enough and perceptive enough to realize in Harley Earl's concept of tail fins that it would bring to the car all the fascination and glamour of aviation. And therefore, add just another thing, another reason for why people wanted to buy automobiles. Not to get back and forth to work but to make believe that they're, you know, flying through the air over Australia, over Europe or whatever in an airplane."

Specifically, the inspiration for the 1948 Cadillac was the Lockheed P-38 fighter plane, which had, among other things, twin tail fins. Earl assigned the members of his styling department to work on a design for a car with fins, but when he presented the idea to other executives at GM, they were appalled. Earl returned to his staff and instructed them to remove the tail fins, but the designer in charge of the project refused. After several days of posturing and debating, the fin was given another chance, and this time it was warmly received. Earl promised to make the fins even bigger the following year, and indeed the public was only too happy to prove him a genius; the 1949 Cadillac was the marque's biggest seller to date.

Predictably, over the next few years, tail fins became all the rage. Oldsmobile added fins in 1949, Buick in 1952, Chrysler in 1955, and even Ford in 1957.

"Coming out of World War II, out of that austere period, I think Americans really wanted to let go," says Bradford Snell. "They wanted something that was wild and frivolous. And the General Motors car with tail fins was precisely what they wanted."

The United States in the 1950s was the richest and most powerful nation in the world. Its citizens—its consumers—were not content with safe, reliable transportation. They craved powerful

(Above) This handsome Roadmaster was the most expensive 1952 Buick model—and those innocent little rails on the trunk were the precursors to the enormous "fin wars" of the 50s. (Top right) The 1951 3/4 ton GMC pickup managed to be both stalwart and awkwardly stylish.

engines and the illusion of luxury in their cars. And Detroit was more than happy to oblige, turning out automobiles that were bigger, faster, more colorful, and more powerful than any produced before or since. In the 1950s gasoline cost only 30 cents a gallon; the price of a basic Chevrolet was $2,000—a significant increase over pre-World War II prices, but still affordable for the typical American family floating along on a wave of economic prosperity unmatched in U.S. history. When Soviet Premier Nikita Khrushchev visited the United States in the 1950s, he was struck by nothing so much as the sight of a factory parking lot, filled to capacity with new automobiles. Khrushchev could not believe that each worker could afford his own car; it was clear evidence of a standard of living that the Soviet Union could not hope to match.

By 1955, sales of passenger cars in the U.S. had reached seven million. In this atmosphere, it seemed as though Detroit could do no wrong; as though there was no design too garish, no fin too large. *Styling* was the language of the time, and no one was more eloquent than Harley Earl. Almost since the day he arrived at GM in 1927, Earl had been effectively applying his stated philosophy of car design: *longer ...lower... wider.* Together with Alfred Sloan, Earl had made planned obsolescence a fact of consumer life in America. By the 1950s, motorists not only tolerated the annual design change, they practically demanded it.

One of the more popular attractions of the period was Harley Earl's Motorama. Introduced in 1952, the Motorama was a traveling promotional

> *THERE ARE so many critics of consumerism today that we can easily forget how wonderful the new gadgets were; how they make life undeniably better for Americans after the war than it had been before it. People lived longer, they had more leisure time, they certainly seemed to be healthier, they were able to send their kids to college, life was better. And this seemed to be what the promise of mass consumer industries, automobility, was all about. A better life.*
>
> *Ron Edsforth*
> *Historian*

Choose your own car climate!

YOU ARE THE WEATHERMAN when your Chevrolet is equipped with Chevrolet's modern all-weather air conditioner and heating system

The popular and dashing Chevrolet Bel Air is shown here in various glamorous permutations including (top inset) 1956, (above) 1958, (left and top and bottom right) and 1955.

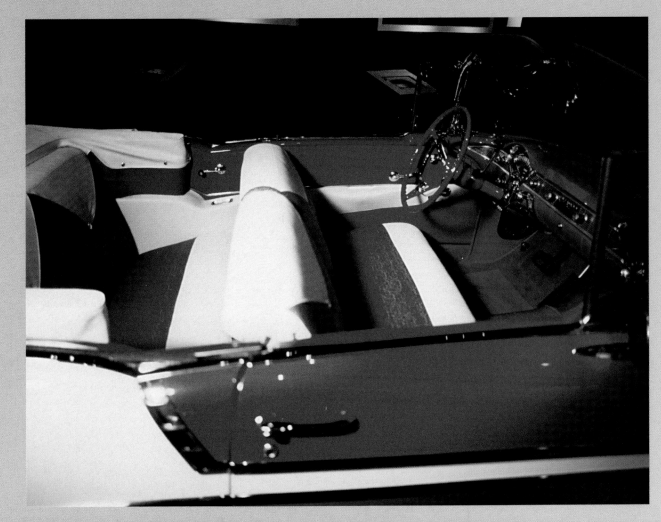

show for General Motors. It started each year at the Waldorf-Astoria in New York before setting off on an extended tour, bringing the latest in GM design and engineering to 10 or 15 major cities across the country.

"At each location we would invite the public to come in and see these new cars and all of the glamour that was associated with the automobile business," remembers Bob Lund. "The Motorama was looked upon by America as being something very, very special, because we were seeing things now that were about to come in the future. It was exciting. In many cases we were looking at cars that contained features you could expect to see in the next car you bought."

And, for most people, there was no hesitation about buying. Consumerism was considered the key to a healthy economy, and as such it was accepted as a way of life by the great majority of

(Below) The 1954 Corvette, designer Harley Earl's stunning dream machine in its second year.

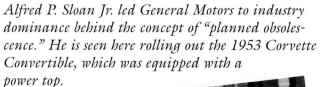

Alfred P. Sloan Jr. led General Motors to industry dominance behind the concept of "planned obsolescence." He is seen here rolling out the 1953 Corvette Convertible, which was equipped with a power top.

Americans. The message as delivered through advertisements and even "educational" public service films, was this: *We will buy our way into prosperity.* The acquisition of material goods—toasters, lawnmowers, television sets, washing machines—was viewed as a healthy and perfectly reasonable way to climb the social ladder; and no single item reflected greater status than the automobile. As a result, sales continued to soar.

Ideologically speaking, consumerism became synonymous with patriotism in the Cold War era of the 1950s. UAW President Walter Reuther even published an article in which he declared that one of the best ways to fight Communism was to build consumerism in the U.S. In that way, the superiority of the capitalist society would be clearly demonstrated to the rest of the world.

"There are so many critics of consumerism today that we can easily forget how wonderful these machines, these new gadgets really were," says Ron Edsforth. "Life was, I think, undeniably better for Americans after the war than it had been before it. People lived longer, they had more leisure time, they certainly seemed to be healthier. And this seemed to be what the promise of mass consumer industries, automobility, was all about. A better life. It's hard for me to accept the idea that buying a car is a patriotic act. But nonetheless, when millions of people did that they certainly generated a kind of prosperity in the economy that was real and important and created the basis for the power of America to confront its enemies in the world. So in that sense I think it's patriotic."

The link between the automobile industry and the perception of patriotism—of the automobile being a vehicle for prosperity and social change—can also be seen in the words and deeds of Charles E. Wilson, who not only went on to become U.S. Secretary of Defense in the Eisenhower administration, but also uttered one of the most famously misquoted lines in U.S. industrial history: "We at General Motors have always felt that what was good for the country was good for General Motors as well." Often, though, Wilson's words are twisted into something else entirely: "*What is good for GM...is good for the country.*"

By the mid-1950s, what was good for GM—and the rest of the automobile industry—was size. Fins kept growing. Chrome was added by the ton. In some cases cars became so heavy and unwieldy that they were difficult to steer. The 1950s was a period of notorious sexual repression, and yet, the cars of this era—with their protuberant bumpers and phallic fins—practically oozed sexuality.

"Automobile design in the 1950s was no longer really about a machine; it was about consumerism," says Alan Hess. "It was about an object of consumption that would fulfill certain desires, above and beyond the pragmatic needs of somebody's life."

The Infamous Ford Edsel

As it turned out, there was a limit to what the motorist would accept. The 1950s will be remembered for giving us some of the finest cars the industry ever produced: the first Corvette (in 1953); the Thunderbird (in 1954). But it will also be remembered for such serious aesthetic blunders as the infamous Ford Edsel of 1957, and the 1959 Cadillac, with its outrageous, almost comical tail fins. Big, self-indulgent cars for a big, self-indulgent time. It was, after all, the 1950s, when nothing succeeded like excess.

Cars for the Stars

(Far left) Richard Burton strikes a typically insouciant pose against his 1957 Cadillac Eldorado. (Left) Cary Grant with—somewhat improbably—a station wagon, his 1955 Ford Country Squire. (Above) "And away we go"...Jackie Gleason seems happy with this new Buick, a birthday gift from his staff.

Sal Mineo and sister Sabrina prepare his 1957 Ford Thunderbird (complete with a Continental kit) for the open road in Oyster Bay, Long Island during the summer of '57.

Fin-tastic! 1959 Cadillac Series 62 Convertible. Cadillac introduced fins in 1948 and made them larger with each succeeding model year. This automotive styling was originally derived from wartime production of tail fins on airplanes, and the trend hit its peak with the soaring fins shown here. The designers responded to the sluggish sales of this car by reducing the fins in following years until they disappeared completely in 1965. (Collection of Anonymous)

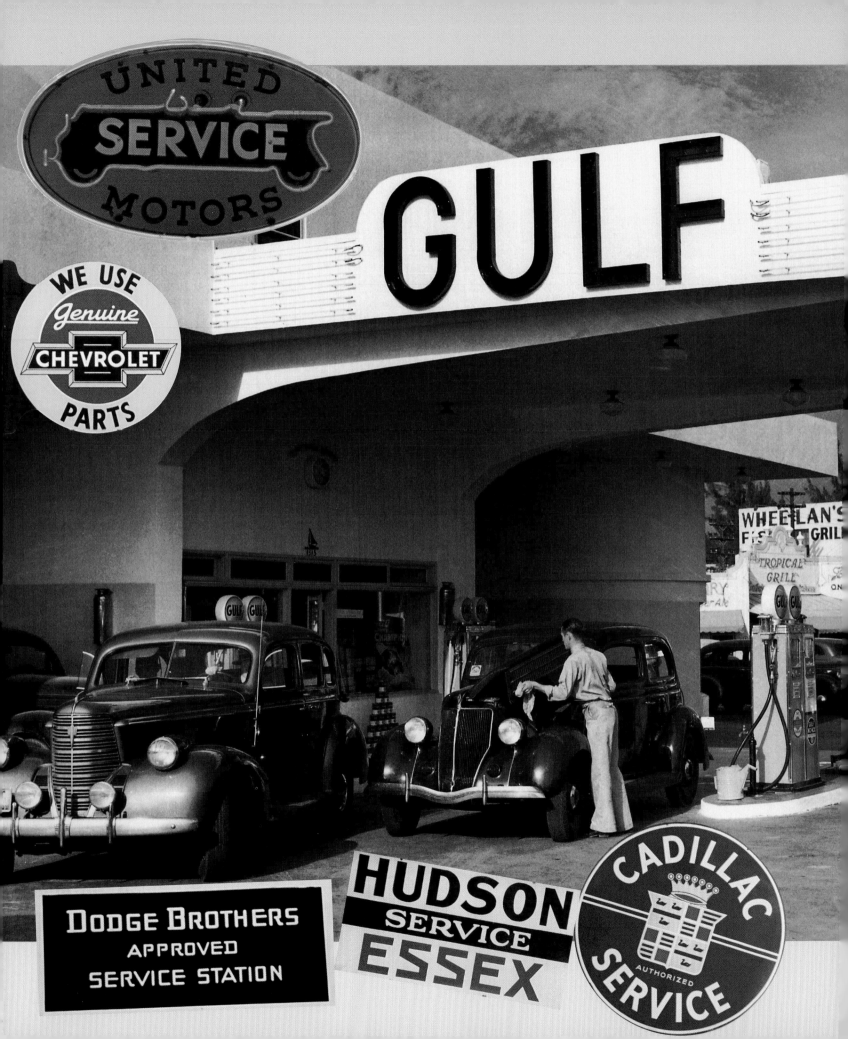

The Open Road

Out of the car culture of the 1950s came a sprawling highway community, similar in theme but larger in scope than the one that was born in the 1920s. As Americans spent more time in their cars, entrepreneurs took notice. And so the Fifties became the "drive-in" decade. Drive-in movie theaters (there were more than 4,000 in the U.S. by 1958), drive-in restaurants, drive-in banks, drive-in churches...even drive-in funeral parlors. Americans, it seemed, never wanted to leave their cars.

Those with the foresight to anticipate this trend were, in many cases, handsomely rewarded. There was a Tennessee real estate developer named Charles Kemmons Wilson, for example. After a

This gas station reflects modern design influences often attributed to the car culture. As the popularity of roadside culture and "drive-in" design became commonplace, a sub-section of familiar artifacts called "automobilia" also arose. These porcelain signs, among other automobilia, have become highly coveted collector's items.

DRIVE IN & SHAVE IN 'JUST A MINUTE'

ELECTRIC SHAVE WHILE·U·WAIT

Late for that important meeting? Drive-in shave outposts expanded—at least for a short time— the choice of services available to the consumer "on the move."

family trip, during which he longed for the comforts of home, Wilson decided to open a string of clean, affordable roadside motels. And thus, in 1951, the Holiday-Inn—the first of the national motel chains—was born.

In 1954 California businessman Ray Kroc visited one of a handful of drive-in restaurants owned by the McDonald brothers, Richard and Maurice, of San Bernardino, California. In the shadow of the first golden arches, surrounded by happy, hungry customers, Kroc experienced an epiphany. He entered into a franchising agreement with the brothers, and within two years he had purchased the fledgling McDonald's chain.

"These fantastic roofs and these ultramodern buildings which were selling hamburgers and milk shakes were created by the automobile," says Alan Hess. "Those neon signs were meant to make the building visible through the windshield of the car, as you're driving by at 40 miles an hour on the street. A building had to grab your attention. And that's what the roadside architecture of the fifties was all about. But it did something more as well. These roadside buildings were one and the same aesthetic as the automobiles of

the 1950s. They were about providing the future right now. They were about providing the goods of technology to the mass audience. They were about speed and efficiency and the joy and the glamour and the beauty of modern materials."

Driving in the 1950s became a national obsession. But there were problems. The end of World War II and the ensuing rush of affluence unleashed a torrent of new cars onto the nation's streets and highways. Within a few short years, as the automobile population exploded (the number of cars on the road doubled between 1945 and 1955—from 26 million to 52 million), these thoroughfares became thick with traffic. At times, it was almost impossible to drive from one side of town to the other. The traffic jam, in all its maddening glory, was becoming common. And drivers were losing their patience.

Federal highway acts in 1912, 1921, and 1944 had all provided subsidies for highway construction. The initial efforts focused on improvements to rural roads—to facilitate the transportation of farm produce to market. (As the car population grew and traffic became

(Right) This restaurant in Harlingen, TX (1939), sends a clear signal as to their specialty. (Below) A novel approach to attracting attention, snow capped roofs in the New Mexico desert along the famous Highway 66 outside Albuquerque (1940).

heavier, busier roads and highways were resurfaced—first with gravel, and later with either concrete or macadam.) States, in turn, were required to match federal dollars. In the 1930s, President Roosevelt's New Deal had made road construction a national priority, and by 1940 major highway construction had begun in Pennsylvania, New York, and, of course, Southern California. In 1946 surfaced road mileage in the United States surpassed non-surfaced road mileage for the first time; twenty years later more than three-quarters of U.S. road mileage would be surfaced.

Los Angeles was one of the great World War II boomtowns, with a population that increased by more than 500,000 between 1940 and 1945. A massive influx of workers was prompted by employment opportunities in the mushrooming defense industry. When the war ended, most of these people stayed; and, since Los Angeles was already becoming a suburban sprawl, nearly all of them were obliged to purchase cars.

The six-lane Arroyo Seco Parkway, completed before the United States' involvement in World War II, was the first step in what would eventually become the most extensive urban freeway system in the world. At a cost of $1.4 million per mile, the Arroyo Seco was also one of the most expensive highways ever produced. It was designed to bring more shoppers into downtown Los Angeles, but instead had just the opposite effect: it allowed

people to escape the city and, for better or worse, established a pattern of suburban development. By the time the highway opened, land values in nearby Pasadena had increased by 25 percent. The Arroyo Seco was designed to carry 45,000 people

Federal highway acts in 1912, 1921, and 1944 provided funds for highway construction. Curiously, however, the rise of our highway system paralleled the decline of certain public transportation options, and an antitrust suit was filed in 1949. (Discussed on pages 170-172.)

(Above) Set aside for the war effort, these "frozen" cars are stored on a Virginia farm (1942). (Below) This crowded trailer camp was built specifically for Farm Security Administration workers at the (1941) Vultee Aircraft Plant in Nashville, TN.

ENTERING
CONNECTICUT
MERRITT PARKWAY

At its best, driving is a form of meditation. It's peaceful, you're moving along at an even flow, the scenery changes around you and so you can be alone with your thoughts, or you can interact with the landscape out there. I particularly love to look at buildings and look at landscapes, look at cities, look at how people live. And the freeways in Los Angeles are one of the best ways to see that. And I've often thought I should have a bumper sticker that says, *Warning, I Brake for Buildings.*

Alan Hess
Historian

ROSE BOWL
MOTOR COURT
AIR COOLED   MODERN   HEATED

SEA BREEZE
TOURIST
VILLAGE

STEAM HEAT

SEA

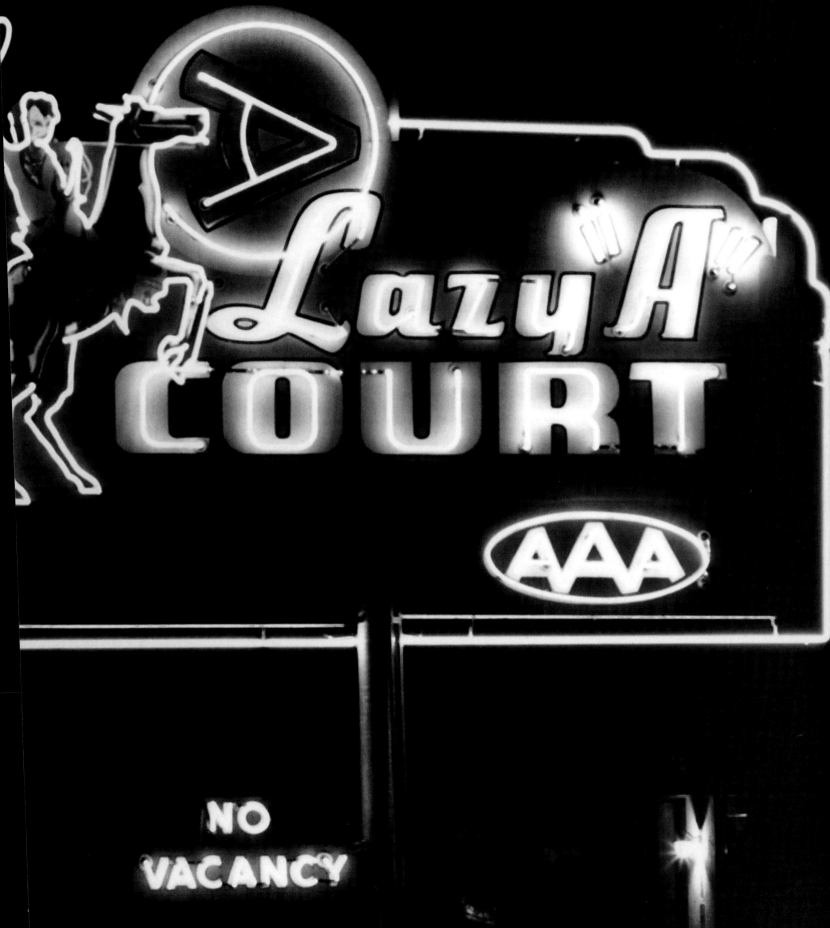

General Motors actually had a very sophisticated corporate message during those years. Because they were the most powerful corporation in the world, they could position themselves as the creator, the provider, and the seer of the future—at the same time, they sold themselves as the All-American, "Heartbeat of America."

Michael Penland
Documentary Screenwriter

a day; within two decades it would be choked with more than 70,000.

And that was merely the beginning. In 1947 the California state legislature authorized construction of a series of expressways between San Francisco and Los Angeles that would ultimately handle more than 40 percent of the state's traffic. California opted for a freeway system in part because it feared a toll system would only exacerbate potential problems associated with traffic jams. Gasoline and vehicle taxes—intended to target the in-state drivers most likely to use the

In the "drive-in decade," drive-through convenience stores (above) were common. And no one who lived in the Fifties can forget their Saturday nights at the malt shop—with rock & roll, cars, food, and plenty of boys and girls, what more could you ask for?

highways—financed a substantial chunk of the project.

"We were coming out of the war, and everybody wanted their wheels," remembers Dave Roper, a retired California highway engineer. "Everybody wanted Southern California. All these veterans who had been through Southern California as part of their Army experience. They all moved from the Midwest and the East, back to California, the Promised Land." But the key was mobility. If you were going to take advantage of the opportunities that Southern California offered—the recreational opportunities, the business opportunities, all of those things—you had to have mobility. Not only for people, but for goods. And the freeway system was the answer to that."

During World War II, federal highway construction had been all but abandoned as the nation turned its attention and resources to the war effort. By the 1950s, the rest of the country was looking at California as its model. As the suburbanization of America continued, new and improved roads were desperately needed. And wanted. At the time, little consideration was given to mass transit. The automobile would not conform to the world around it; the world would be reshaped to accommodate the automobile.

"By the end of the Twenties, the highway program had been accepted by the general public as essential," says highway engineer Frank Turner. "Everybody was automotive minded. Highways were the way you got there. That was the way you became an individual in the community. So there was great pressure for rapid improvement of the highway system, enlargement of the system, and to improve it to the point that everybody would have a good road wherever he wanted to go. It was considered one of the citizen's rights, so to speak. An American citizen would have the right to go anywhere, anytime, at his own speed in his own vehicle, by his own mode, and that would be by car. But he had to have a road to do that."

Automobile manufacturers were not blind to the desires and concerns of their constituency. Fearful that the motorist might begin to view driving as an unpleasant experience, and thus be less inclined to purchase a new car, the Big Three started lobbying for more highway construction. General Motors, as the industry's dominant corporation, assumed a position of leadership.

"GM in the 1950s certainly had a very large role in shaping public policy," says Harley Shaiken. "GM may have been in the business of building cars, but as a corporation GM wanted to insure that there would be an infrastructure for those cars to exist in, and an infrastructure that encouraged more and more people to buy cars. And nowhere was this more important than the interstate highway system."

The Interstate Highway Act of 1956 authorized the construction of a nationwide system of toll-free superhighways. Encompassing some 41,000 miles of highway, at an estimated cost of $27 billion (within 10 years the projected cost would be doubled), it was easily the largest public-works project in history. A whopping 90 percent of the funding for this project would come from the federal government, presumably through gasoline and use taxes. Perhaps more interesting than the project itself, though, is the story behind its birth—a story that vividly illustrates the link between government and big business, and the power of the automobile industry in the 1950s; specifically, the power of General Motors.

As early as the 1920s Alfred P. Sloan had identified and treated the problem of market saturation. He understood that a certain degree of manipulation was required if business was to remain healthy. The auto industry could not simply rely on customers who traded in their cars every five to seven years. The market had to be broadened.

Sloan accomplished this in a number of ways. First, by encouraging highway construction at the expense of rail expansion and repair, and second, through the concept of planned obsolescence. In 1932 he traveled to Washington and established the National Highway Users Conference, which was comprised of several trade groups—tire manufacturers, automobile manufacturers, oil companies—that would be adversely affected by the elimination of road construction. These businesses formed a powerful lobby that managed to earmark gas tax revenues in such a way that they simply could not be used for any purpose other than highway construction.

In the 1940s Sloan intensified his campaign against the railways by organizing a holding company called National City Lines. His partners in the venture were other suppliers of automotive products: Standard Oil of California, Phillips Petroleum, and Firestone Tire. The goal of National City Lines was simple and ruthless: purchase streetcar companies, shut down their lines, and replace them with buses—GM buses fueled by Standard Oil gasoline (on the West Coast) or Phillips Petroleum gasoline (on the East Coast), and equipped with Firestone tires. National City

Lines acquired the Los Angeles Railway, a local streetcar system, in 1944, as well as pieces of the larger Pacific Electric Railway. Soon both rail systems were replaced by GM buses.

"General Motors desperately wanted to somehow decrease the influence of the electric railway interest as a competitor of the automobile," Snell adds. "They had to get rid of streetcars. One way they were trying to do this was through freight leverage with the railroads, because some of the railroads owned some of the largest street railway companies in the country—in New York, in Connecticut, in California, and other places. And through finance. By going to the banks that were involved with the street railway companies, General Motors was putting financial leverage on the banks to cut off the credit to these companies. Finally, if these measures didn't work, General Motors resorted to just buying them up."

In 1949 National City Lines and the organizations behind it—General Motors, Standard Oil of California, Phillips Petroleum, and Firestone Tire—were all found guilty of violating antitrust laws. Each of the corporations was fined $5,000; the corporate officials involved were each fined precisely one dollar. To the end, they vehemently denied that their intent was to eliminate the rail lines.

"I've interviewed the lawyers involved in bringing that suit and I've looked at the draft indictments," says Bradford Snell. "It was understood by everyone involved, including the defense, that the object of the conspiracy was to eliminate the streetcars, the electric rail transportation. But the violation, obviously, was in the monopolization of the products that were put in as substitutes for the railway system."

Regardless of the intent, the upshot of all this maneuvering was an increase in automobile traffic and a decrease in the use of mass transit.

"Ultimately, because no one really wanted to ride these buses—I mean, whenever you put in buses in place of the railways, patronage declines precipitously—[GM] would dump the buses onto the city, sell them back to the city as a bankrupt operation," Snell says. "Then they'd take the money from that and use it in a revolving fund to buy up other streetcar systems."

By the 1950s it was generally accepted that the

Suburban sprawl, Southern California, mid-Fifties

automobile had become an enormously effective economic tool. If the American consumer wanted to buy a new home in the suburbs, he needed not only a car to get there, but also a road on which to travel. The automobile industry appeared to be nothing less than the key to sustained prosperity. That the paving of America and the eruption of the suburbs would eventually lead to the demise of the American city and prompt isolation and class division on a grand scale was not factored into the equation. At the time, highway expansion meant growth. It meant jobs. It meant money. For the Big Three, it was a multibillion-dollar subsidy.

"The Fifties were a very different climate with

the inauguration of Eisenhower as president," says Bradford Snell. "You had an extremely pro-business and pro-automotive administration. When Charles Wilson, formerly president of General Motors, moved in as Secretary of Defense, bringing with him all the General Motors people down to the Pentagon; when other Cabinet posts were filled up and undersecretary positions were filled by General Motors personnel, you in essence had a cabinet that if not favorable towards General Motors, was certainly not resistant to any of their overtures."

Eisenhower established the Clay Commission to write the new highway legislation. That Lucius Clay, who headed the commission, was on the General Motors board of directors barely raised an eyebrow. Nor did it seem to matter that he was working closely with Charles Wilson. No one even suggested the possibility of a conflict of interest.

"Clay was the key person behind drafting Eisenhower and running him as a Republican candidate in the 1952 election," notes Snell. "And at that point, of course, Clay was already in with General Motors and was privy to all the interstate highway system plans. So it was almost inevitable that when Eisenhower was inaugurated and got into office and Sloan brought down the plans, that Clay would be named head of the committee to investigate the merits of this measure.

"I believe the Clay committee had just two days of hearings. It was a *fait accompli*. It was something that General Motors wished to have. And Eisenhower was totally in favor of it. It was something that was going to happen."

Postwar highway expansion, not coincidentally, was parallelled by the growth of suburbia. The suburban population in the United States increased by nearly 50 percent in the 1950s, changing forever the way Americans lived and worked. Unlike the denizens of the first suburbs, which sprouted shortly after the turn of

The advent of a drive-in society changed life in many ways—some for the better, and others... only time will tell. These two teenagers find a way to unwind in their automobile at a drive-in movie.

the century, suburbanites of the 1950s tended not to live along trolley or rail lines, which funneled neatly into city centers. Instead, they took up residence in manufactured communities far from the urban crush.

And they never looked back.

By the late 1950s the federal government was spending billions of dollars annually on highway construction; the highways, of course, gave motorists easier access to the suburbs, which in turn fueled a housing boom. Once, automobile ownership was considered the cornerstone of the American Dream; now, home ownership—preferably a single-family home on a quarter-acre of land in a bucolic suburban setting—became synonymous with the American Dream.

"The suburbs in the 1950s are clearly a place where middle-class people or working-class people are seeking a better life, a life they perceive to be better than the life in the cities," says Ron Edsforth. "It's important to remember that most of these people had grown up in housing that was old, that was rundown, that was crowded and cramped, that didn't have all the amenities that the homes of the 1950s had. So they were very desirable living spaces, seemingly much more open, bright, healthier than the places they were leaving in the cities. What you get in the development of the suburbs in the 1950s is not simply a sense of escaping from something awful—which I don't think is the case, because there are regrets about leaving the old neighborhoods in the cities—but the moving to something that's so magnetic because it's so much better that it can't be resisted. You know, 'This is a place where I want to raise my kids because this is a place where they will definitely have a better life than the life I'm leaving behind.'"

Perhaps no American cultural phenomenon has prompted so much heated debate as the growth of suburbia. Advocates stress quality-of-life issues: better schools, cleaner air, less crime, privacy. Critics argue that the flight to the suburbs has been anathema to many cities and has fostered a cold, impersonal society of lonely, overstressed, overworked people who are now slaves to the highways and automobiles they once cherished.

An aerial photograph of Lakewood, California in 1950. Many negative aspects of suburbia—notably conformity, separation from true cities (and everything they offer), and a sense of drabness—have complicated the allure of these "safe, clean, mini-utopias."

and easy to get to, and it has exploded them and smeared them out over the landscape. And this new suburban landscape that we have created has none of the characteristics of a town or city and none of the characteristics of the country."

The sociopolitical implications of the suburbs were not really of any great concern to the automobile industry. To Detroit, the suburbs represented a vast new market, and they were embraced as such. The automobile companies began to promote the idea

Levittown houses (shown above in 1977) still reflect their common origin—and the residents seem to like it that way. Fairless, Pennsylvania (below), grew up in 1951 at the rate of sixteen houses per day.

"Suburbia has had a tremendously damaging effect on the civic life of our country," says James Kunstler. "What suburbia has done is taken all the activities of our lives and dispersed them into separate pods which we are compelled to drive to. So, first of all, it's fantastically expensive to use suburbia on an everyday basis. And it has taken what were once integral neighborhoods and cities, in which the different activities were all interlinked

that each family needed a car...or two cars. Maybe three. Dad needed a car to drive to work; mom needed a car to chaperone the kids to school or baseball practice, and to do the grocery shopping. And, eventually, as the children became teenagers, with social lives of their own, they too would need wheels. Americans bought into this philosophy, in large part because it was absolutely true. Families in the suburbs really did need more than one car.

And by 1960 statistics reflected this fact: nearly one-third of American households owned at least two cars.

Nevertheless, Frank Turner argues, "We didn't create suburbia by putting in a road. It's the other way around. Suburbia came along because people didn't want to live downtown. They could and did move out somewhere else. Virtually all of those suburbs were developed long before there was a road out there. And that's the first bitching that the suburban residents came up with: 'Hey, we can't get to town here. This road's terrible. It's blocked and jammed and everything.' Well, we didn't move them out there. They came to us after the fact and said we need transportation."

Whether the highway gave rise to the suburbs or the suburbs gave rise to the highway is a point of contention. What cannot be debated, however, is that both are byproducts of the automobile.

It's true that the United States suffered from a severe housing shortage immediately after World War II. Soldiers returning home were often forced to move in with relatives. Public pressure, coupled with the ensuing baby boom, sparked federal housing policies that gave millions of Americans access to guaranteed home loans.

> I can fix a housing problem, or a race problem, but I can't do both.
> *William Levitt*
> *Builder*

But where and how would these homes be built? A New York contractor named William Levitt turned out to be an important player in this evolving drama. Levitt and Sons had built Navy housing as part of the war effort, but it would be the postwar housing shortage that allowed the company to develop its unique approach to building single-family homes; an approach not unlike the assembly-line model of Detroit. By applying Henry Ford's theories of mass production and division of labor to home construction, Levitt and Sons would build 40 homes a day in the potato fields of Long Island, 30 miles from New York. The project, known as Levittown, provided new, affordable housing for 17,000 families. The cookie-cutter homes lacked character and individuality. They were, however, neat and clean, and eager middle-class consumers were quick to snatch them up.

"William Levitt became a symbol of the ability for American industry to produce in quantity and in quality what was needed for a massive and favored part of our population at that time," says Levitt's son, Bill Levitt, who worked as a laborer on the Levittown project. "In other words, basic but good housing. Levittown changed America more than it simply changed the New York metro-

politan scene, because it became the standard against which all housing development was measured over the following ten years—a couple of decades, even. It became the standard by which legislators in Washington enacted new programs to make it possible for people everywhere in the United States to purchase housing. And because one could see that it was possible, all over the country people demanded—literally *demanded*— the right to live in the country rather than in the cities in which they had lived for generations."

Suburbia changed more than the geographic landscape; it also changed the social landscape. Lifelong city residents suddenly discovered that for roughly the same amount of money they had been paying for rent, it was possible to move to the suburbs. Theoretically, they would have access to all the advantages of country living, yet still be within a fairly easy commute of the city—which was where the jobs remained. Many of the original Levittown residents bought their first new cars along with their first new homes.

Unfortunately, what new suburbanites often experienced was not the exhilaration of space and privacy they had anticipated, but rather a feeling of isolation. This was particularly true of women; young housewives and mothers who were left alone while their husbands went off to work. The solution to this sensation of entrapment, of course, was a second car. By the end of the 1950s women were beginning to confront the very rigid, stereotypical roles they had been compelled to inhabit in the past. The automobile, for them, became a vehicle for social mobility. Yes, it helped them complete the most fundamental household tasks, such as shopping and banking. But it also allowed them to have lives outside the home. It even gave them access to the first women's liberation meetings.

It gave them freedom.

But freedom had a price.

"In the 1950s, how we lived was being redefined," says Harley Shaiken. "The promise was you could move away from the city to the suburb. The reality was you moved from the city to the traffic jam. And in a way that's the story of the automobile in the Fifties. For the individual, the dream was realized. But when everyone began doing it, the dream had a different character."

I was working as a common laborer on a landscape gang in the summer of 48, at the age of sixteen. And the impression of activity was just overwhelming. I believe that the company built 5,200 houses within one calendar year in Levittown, Long Island, New York. And for two-and-a-half months I was working on what probably were seven or eight hundred houses worth of landscaping, with the same crew day in and day out and watching all the other crews of the other trades move from house to house to house. This was the exact opposite of an automobile assembly line, where the automobiles move and the workers stay in the same place. Here, the product stayed stationary and static and the workers moved from product to product. And it was a system that was finely honed....And it worked to a tee.

Bill Levitt, Jr.
Builder

Part Three

Car Wars

CHAPTER 8

Lean and Mean

Nineteen fifty five was a remarkable year for the automotive industry, a year of exceptional profitability and innovation. In terms of design and technology, it was also an intensely exciting year. For the first time, powerful V-8 engines were installed in Chevrolets, Plymouths, and other low-priced cars. The consumer could choose from a vast array of colors, styles, and prices. Most important of all, though, he or she had access to power.

Internally, the '55 Chevy—known as the "Hot One"—was modeled after the larger General Motors cars, most notably the Cadillac. It was equipped with a 265-cubic-inch engine, a precursor to the muscle cars of the Sixties. It was lightweight, small, and powerful, and it helped make 1955 the single most

Americans were privileged to enjoy a great variety of vehicles in the Fifties. Performance—particularly speed—became a premium, as more auto makers added V-8 engines and more horsepower to their cars. Garages would soon feature a great diversity, such as this 1961 Cadillac Series 62 Short-Deck Sedan and 1948 Volkswagen Porsche. (Collection of the Natural History Museum of Los Angeles County; Porsche—Collection of Monty Montgomery)

Cars were one of the main engines of change in the culture in the 1950s...a major element of the youth culture which also included rock and roll music, a new way of dressing, a whole new relationship between children and adults. The landscape was altered.

When you think of the image of James Dean, a movie star, a youth movie star, a young man, living his lifestyle in a Porsche, a dream car, and doing what those cars are made for, which is speeding...and then he died in that car. You have all the major elements that can make an icon. You have youth. You have celebrity. You have a spectacular car. You have speed. And when all those come together in such a dramatic way as, of course, a death, you do have the makings of myth.

James Dean's death in a car crash, when he was speeding, sums up, really, the power of the car in the culture in the 1950s.

Alan Hess
Historian

productive year to date in U.S. automobile history. At the same time that Harley Earl was designing cars that were longer, lower, and wider, Detroit was now offering cars that were...*faster*.

It was, by most accounts, the beginning of a new automotive craze—the horsepower race. Long after the styling excesses of the 1950s had lost their appeal, the zest for power would continue to be sustained by a youthful and enthusiastic cult of hot-rodders—grease-stained kids who loved to cruise and race, and whose icon was the young film star James Dean, who died in September 1955 when he lost control of his speeding Porsche Spyder.

Over the next 15 years Detroit did its best to accommodate this comparatively small but influential segment of the market. The neighborhood gearhead could spend hours in his garage, tearing apart an old Ford coupe and customizing it with a bored-out V-8 from the '50s...or he could simply walk into a showroom and purchase a brand new muscle car. By the mid-1960s the choices were dazzling: the 389-cubic-inch Pontiac GTO (named after Ferrari's Gran Turismo Omologato), designed by an engineer named John Z. DeLorean; the Olds 442 (4-barrel carburetor, 4-on-the-floor, 2 exhausts); the Chevy Malibu SS; the Plymouth Barracuda.

The Corvette's fiberglass shell enabled Chevrolet to introduce a sporty new look to American cars, but in spite of the car's breathtaking design, it was criticized for having little under the hood. (Below) Along with the Cord Sportsman series, the Edsel Ford-inspired Lincoln Continentals are considered one of the two most beautiful American production cars ever. This 1956 Lincoln Continental Mark II lives up to that tradition. Just ask Elvis Presley. The King of Rock was also the King of Cars. His Mark II was one of the first in his hundred-plus collection.

The 1957 Chevrolet Bel Air Sport Coupe was one of the most desirable cars in America with its hard top styling, muscular build, and a powerful V-8 that rocked the low-priced market.

Many of these cars had an insatiable thirst for gasoline (five miles a gallon was not uncommon), but their owners didn't mind; they weren't concerned with economy—they were concerned with power. These machines were made for racing—on deserted city streets, back roads, and airport runways—not sightseeing. They were for daring young speed junkies who lived in their garages and devoured every issue of such publications as *Hot Rod, Car and Driver, Road and Track,* and *Rod and Custom;* kids who found their anthems in such

songs as "Maybelline," "GTO," and "Little Deuce Coupe." They were not for everyone, but they were certainly popular enough (more than 60,000 GTOs were sold between 1964 and 1965) to justify their existence.

Pervasive as it was, the youth culture of the late 1950s and 1960s did not define the automobile industry. Even as Detroit was unveiling its first muscle car, the winds of change were blowing.

"In 1955, the American dream was seated in vinyl and had a panoramic windshield and three

colors on the very same car," says Harley Shaiken. "By 1955, we were looking towardsthe '60s, not back to the '40s. The cars of that year—the Ford, the Chevy, the Plymouth, from the low end to the top end, the Cadillacs, the Lincolns, and the Chryslers, the luxury, the vinyl, the pillarless hardtops, and all the other gizmos that Detroit could manufacture—defined what the future would look like. In the mid-1950s luxury for the masses had arrived. You needed larger engines just to carry the chrome."

The engines would continue to get bigger, but soon the cars were getting smaller. By 1957—a recession year—the inevitable backlash had begun. In the midst of the Cold War, the launching of Sputnik by the Soviet Union prompted much hand-wringing and soul-searching in the United States. Though it was not really a major technological breakthrough, Sputnik was a blow to the national psyche. Social critics, naturally, were quick to vilify consumerism; priorities, they said, were not in order. The American public seemed to

agree, and soon Detroit was producing smaller, more economical cars.

"When the Russians launched Sputnik, a real shock ran through the country," says Ron Edsforth. "I can remember being in grammar school and this being a major issue in our classes and our teachers telling us we were just going to have to really get to work and really apply ourselves because now it was clear the Soviet Union could do things that we couldn't do and that we had to catch up with them. And I think that this called into question, at least in part, the sort of self-indulgent materialism that you see expressed in the chrome dinosaurs, as they're sometimes called—the cars of the late 1950s; that these excesses had maybe steered us away from what was really necessary to win what was really important, and that was the Cold War against the Soviet Union."

One of the victims of this transitional period was the notorious Ford Edsel. Planning for the most famous flop in automotive history began in 1948, when Henry Ford II deter-

The Thunderbird (below) was Ford's first full-fledged sports car and an instant classic. You don't need to be a collector to fall in love with this mint condition T-bird, circa 1957. It's easy to see why early T-birds (1954-57) are among the most sought after vintage cars on the planet.

The Edsel existed in '58, '59 and '60. It was really a terrific car, though the styling was in some people's views a little bit radical. And today that's the reason it makes quite a collector car. It was way ahead of its time, but was brought out in a time when the market was looking for smaller cars and the economy wasn't the greatest for that large a car. The timing wasn't right.

I have one on the lot that is over 21 feet long. It handles and goes great. When you're going down the road everybody takes a look at it because it's so different. Many manufacturers have copied a lot of the styling of this car...but years later. The Edsel was just ahead of its time. It was and is a dynamic car.

I thought they were beautiful. And to this day I think they're beautiful. The Edsel got a lot of bad raps from people.

Dave Duncan
Ford auto dealer

The Edsel (shown here with its equally gaudy convertible) is perhaps the most famous bomb in manufacturing history, causing Ford to lose $250 million in 1958 alone. It was said by critics to resemble an Oldsmobile sucking on a lemon.

1958

1960 Edsel

mined that his company needed a new and dramatic entry in the competitive field of moderately priced cars. Far from being the offspring of some misguided, impulsive executive, the Edsel was the first American automobile whose design was based on extensive market research.

The project was shelved for several years during the Korean War, but resurrected under the guidance of stylist Roy Brown. By 1955 the design had been approved by top management at the Ford Motor Company, and soon the new marque was ready for production. Unfortunately, it still did not have a moniker. After hundreds of others were discarded, board chairman Ernest R. Breech recommended naming the new model after Henry Ford's late son.

On September 4, 1957, the Ford Edsel was introduced. There were four lines: the Corsair and Citation (each with a massive 345-horsepower engine), and the slightly smaller Ranger and Pacer. Across the board, response to the Edsel was, to put it mildly, cool. On the subject of handling and performance, automotive critics were split. *Motor Trend* gave the Edsel good marks, while *Consumer Reports* savaged the car. But it was the appearance of the Edsel that provoked the most bilious response. Some critics com-

189

FORD THUNDERBIRD '59

The car everyone would love to own!

In 1958, when a neighbor drove down the block in his spanking new Chevy Impala Sport Coupe (above), bicycles were dumped, stick ball games abandoned, and hoses shut off in order to gape and congratulate the new owner. Few were surprised if that same owner was still driving it 10 years later.

With fins that could rival a cartoon rocket, the 1959 Cadillac Eldorado (below) looks ready to blast off. Sales didn't and the industry shortly did away with the tail fin concept to widespread consumer approval. By 1959, the Ford Thunderbird (left) had become one of the most desired status symbols in suburbia.

THEIR BOATS ARE DIFFERENT, BUT THEY BOTH DRIVE PLYMOUTHS

One man owns an outboard, the other owns a cruiser. They are equally proud of their identical '59 Plymouths, for Plymouth offers nearly everything *anyone* could want.

Here's a low-price car that gives a lap-of-luxury ride: Torsion-Aire, at no additional cost. Alone in its class, Plymouth offers outstanding optional advances like Swivel Seats, Push-

Button Driving and rear Sport Deck. Its styling is clean and in good taste. And Plymouth economy is indisputable.

In America's recognized competitive test for gasoline economy, the Mobilgas Economy Run, Plymouth won its class with 21.15 miles per gallon. Why not get aboard Plymouth at *your* dealer's soon?

d at Jordan Marsh Yacht Landing, Miami, Florida　　Plymouth Division of Chrysler Corporation

Plymouth
to be fully appreciated, must be driven

pared its grille to a toilet seat or a horse collar; others said it resembled a man sucking a lemon.

"From a design standpoint, the Edsel was kind of a conglomeration of all the cliches that we were working with during that time," says Chuck Jordan, who was then a young designer for General Motors. "There was chrome and all these weird graphic patterns on the car. And that vertical grille did not capture anybody's imagination. It just was repulsive. It didn't look good in any way, shape, or form, or under any light. It really was far from an outstanding design. In fact, in many ways it was ugly, and ugly is not what designers stand for."

It didn't help that the Edsel was not a cheap car. In the two years that it took the Edsel to go from drawing board to showroom, Americans had begun to examine price tags a bit more closely. By late 1957, the Edsel was seen as an extravagance—and an unappealing extravagance at that. All of this was bad news for Ford, which needed to sell at least 200,000 Edsels in the first year just to break even. That did not come close to happening. Although improvements were made the following year, the car's fate was sealed. When production ceased on November 19, 1959, approximately 110,000 Edsels had been sold. History has gen-

Advertisements for the 1959 Plymouth Fury reinforced the universal appeal of this competent car—which featured great fins and sharp whitewall tires.

193

*E*ven mid-list cars from the Fifties and early Sixties seem to exude a certain mystique. The low profile, tasteful chrome, and aerodynamic fins of this 1960 Buick are representative of what many consider the definitive era of American cars.

Marketing campaigns come from the top down: This cover from the 1961 Plymouth Fury dealer catalog features a spectacular scene of a sunset on a deserted, wind-swept beach and a couple enjoying the solitude their Fury has afforded them.

erally been unkind to the car, though it does have its advocates.

"Personally, I think the Edsel has been given a bum rap in many ways," says Alan Hess. "The design was really quite marvelous in its use of different Fifties forms: swoops, angles, tricolored cars, all brought together…especially with that marvelous oval form on the front.

"But the Edsel did become synonymous with the ultimate excess of Detroit in the 1950s. Here was a car which was supposed to be all new, had all of the latest elements for a car, and yet it failed. It bombed. And that's indisputable. As a result, it took on a larger life than that of the ordinary failed car model. It became a whipping boy for the 1950s."

If the Edsel was the most famous casualty of the 1950s, it was hardly the only one. By the end of the decade most of the independents had faded from the scene. A notable survivor was American Motors, which sold an astounding 217,000 Ramblers in 1958, and twice that many in 1960. The success of the Rambler, a small, economical car, gave executives at the Big Three pause. Already in 1958 the tiny, peculiar Volkswagen Beetle had captured a five percent share of the market. Suddenly it seemed as though the conventional wisdom coming out of Detroit—that Americans wanted only big, luxurious, powerful cars—was seriously flawed.

The Big Three began scrambling. By the time the outrageously ostentatious 1959 Cadillac, with its massive fins, was released, designers in Detroit knew the chrome revolution of the 1950s was over. Already they were hard at work, preparing 1960 models that would be smaller, more sensible. At GM, styling wizard Harley Earl was on the brink of retirement; a new generation of designers and engineers would shape the next decade of automobile culture.

Pontiac dealer literature features the appropriately titled Safari station wagon, again encouraging Americans to utilize their automobiles to enhance their lifestyles.

The legendary 1964 Ford Mustang coupe started the "pony car revolution," proving once and for all that bigger is not always better.

I was on a very small handpicked team that designed the first Mustang. It was the most exciting project I think I ever had. The car was just, it was just magic. It had the right proportions. It had the right style. There was nothing like it on the road.

There are designs that just sort of sit there and there are other designs that really excite people and make them want to buy. Nobody can really explain how it happens or how it gets there, but you do know it when you see it. It's there. It's magical. It's an emotional experience that the designers feel and that the customer feels when they see the design.

We didn't know it would be as successful as it was and we didn't know it would have the staying power that it has today. I think the main reason that the Mustang is doing so well today is because we kept that same magic, if you will, those ingredients, those strong Mustang cues, bold mouth, the scoop on the side, the triple tail lamps, the dual cockpit interior. We evolved the car and updated it and the car still maintains itself.

Jack Telnack
Automotive designer

"They say we overcooked. Okay, maybe we overcooked. But we started fixing it the very next year, 1960," notes Chuck Jordan. "And we believed in what we were doing. We believed that the direction we were going in was right. We were designing commercial products. Automobiles to be desired and sold to the customer. We weren't doing museum pieces. And we weren't doing theoretical things. We were every year doing some new cars that people wanted."

To combat the increasing popularity of foreign imports, the Big Three began turning out a variety of compact cars. Chrysler offered the Valiant; GM unveiled the Tempest and Chevy II; Ford had the Comet and Falcon—and the Mustang.

Nothing out of Detroit in the 1960s was more warmly received than the Mustang, Ford's version of the sporty little "pony car." Released in 1964, the Mustang was an instant success (it appeared on the covers of both *Time* and *Newsweek*). The car was relatively inexpensive, fun to drive, and, perhaps most

Stars continued in the parade of vehicles: Annette Funicello gracefully disembarks from a 1956 Ford Thunderbird.

The VW Bug was very alarming to Detroit, but alarming from the sense of complete confidence. The fact that the bug captured 5% of the market Detroit took very seriously, but it seemed to be a peculiar 5% of the market. It wasn't those people that turned out in droves to see the introductions of the new models every September. These were people who were marching to a different drummer.

Harley Shaiken
Historian

Based on a sketch by Hitler (inspired by the beetle), the Volkswagen ("people's car") outsold the Model T and is still being manufactured in Mexico in its original design. This 1964 version, however, has one major innovation—a sun roof.

important of all, looked great. With its long hood and tight rear, the Mustang had the appearance of a sports car. But its popularity easily transcended the gearhead crowd. More than half a million Mustangs were sold in 1965, and soon it became one of the most copied cars in the business.

"The Mustang was a much more concise, smaller car, and it came out at a time when we were probably starting to get into this change of attitude in the United States," remembers Jack Telnack, Ford's vice president of design. "We were ready to accept something else. And we thought that, you know, maybe bigness isn't the only answer out there anymore. There are other things in an automobile that are much more desirable."

The Mustang stood out at a time when Detroit was offering an impressive, if somewhat bewildering menu of automobiles. Compacts dominated

the market, to be sure, but there was a concerted effort to be all things to all people. In the Fifties it was presumed that motorists wanted big, flashy cars; in the Sixties there was no real presumption. Consumers demonstrated with their checkbooks that the demand for compact cars had been too long ignored. But Big Three executives were not about to abandon the luxury market completely.

As a result, the 1960s saw a proliferation of models and marques unparalleled in automotive history.

But even as automakers were trying to demonstrate their versatility, and even as the Mustang began its long and impressive journey into automotive history, consumer dissatisfaction was mounting. Critics of the automobile blasted the self-indulgent excesses of the 1950s. They pointed out a rather obvious correlation between highway expansion and an increase in traffic-related deaths. In sum, they painted a picture of the automobile not as a great emancipator, but rather as a gas-guzzling, pollution-spewing instrument of mayhem.

It didn't help Detroit any that just as this movement was picking up steam, in 1965, a young lawyer and consumer advocate named Ralph Nader published a book titled *Unsafe at Any Speed: The Designed-in Dangers of the American Automobile*. The book, which became a bestseller and something of a counter-culture bible, took the automobile industry to task for, among other things, "insisting on maintaining the freedom to rank safety anywhere it pleases on its list of considerations."

Nader's sharpest attack was reserved for General Motors and its Chevrolet Corvair, an interesting though temperamental little car that had been introduced in 1959. The compact Corvair featured an air-cooled rear engine patterned after the VW Beetle's. It was a truly innovative car, unlike anything Detroit was producing at the time. Unfortunately, the car was also inherently unstable. It required far more of its driver than the typical American car—a fact that prompted *Car and Driver* to label the Corvair, "one of the nastiest-handling cars ever built."

Historian David Lewis, who worked in public

The sporty Chevrolet Corvair (1964, left and inset) initially had major design imperfections which made the vehicle dangerous to drive. Ralph Nader wrote a book on the problem, which prompted Chevy to fix newer models and inspired Americans to become consumer watchdogs.

Some tigers are fierce. Some tigers are ferocious. We build both.

It's getting so that choosing between our Wide-Track Tigers is as distressing as it is enjoyable. For instance, should you choose the incredible GTO with its extra helping of horsepower (360), or the way it comes (335)? Or should you go for the Le Mans with a 285-hp V-8, a 250-hp V-8, or 140-hp six? Either way they're all tigers with bucket seats, carpeting and lots of Oh-you-kid! **Quick Wide-Track Tigers Pontiac Le Mans & GTO**

The 1964 Pontiac Tempest GTO Coupe with a 389 hp V-8 is considered the first "muscle car." It could take a Ferrari in a drag race. Not bad at about one-sixth the cost.

relations for GM at the time, vividly remembers hearing of the car's design flaws.

"There were many one-car accidents in Corvairs. And General Motors knew this definitely as early as 1961, but chose not to make a public announcement of it nor to have any recalls," Lewis says. "I happened to be secretary of the Public Relations Planning Committee in 1961. At that time, during a meeting, the number two man in public relations, Bill Hamilton, rushed back from the GM tech center and said that GM's engineers had confirmed what had been talked about, that Corvairs were inherently unsafe because of the design of the suspension system. And I remember that one of the people at the meeting asked, 'Well, what are we going to do about it?' And Hamilton said, 'The lawyers say we're not going to do anything about it. We're going to ride it out.' That information, however, was kept under wraps. There was no government mandate to recall the cars for safety reasons and so nothing was done. It was one of the most socially irresponsible acts by an industrial firm of the 20th century."

Chrysler Corporation president Robert Lutz, who was both a GM employee and a satisfied Corvair owner in the early 1960s, is much less harsh in his assessment.

"There was nothing fundamentally wrong with

The Cobra (and muscle cars in general) are uncompromisingly designed for performance and excitement and don't much care how good the top is or whether you get wind buffeting or not. In other words, there is very little effort expended on making the car truly refined or useful. And all of the effort is focused on performance, braking, handling, steering, and so forth.

It's about speed, power, and the raw thrill of driving a car that has almost unlimited horsepower. At any time, whenever you need power, it's there. It's sort of the vehicular equivalent of having unlimited money and you can just sign checks all day.

Needless to say, it becomes very difficult to obey all of the nation's speed laws in these....

Robert Lutz
President of Chrysler

The 1965 Plymouth Barracuda, GM's answer to the Ford Mustang, was a small, fast, and relatively inexpensive sports car, making it popular with young men.

Fourteen years after the first Corvette Sport Coupe was introduced, the 1967 Sting Ray (left) still had style, as did its older brother, the 1966 Sting Ray (below).

Chevrolet produced an experimental Mako Shark II in the mid-60s, which was toured and touted around the nation. It was indeed ahead of its time, however, as no production Sharks were ever manufactured. Some style points were incorporated into the 70s' Corvettes, though.

Many Americans insist on personalizing, or "customizing," their vehicles for added aesthetics and/or performance. This 1932 Ford "Hi-Boy Roadster" is based on a 1932 Ford frame, but uses a 1929 body and a custom hood. The mid-century modifications to this car have remained untouched, making it a rare example of early 1950's hot-rodding. (Collection of the Natural History Museum of Los Angeles County)

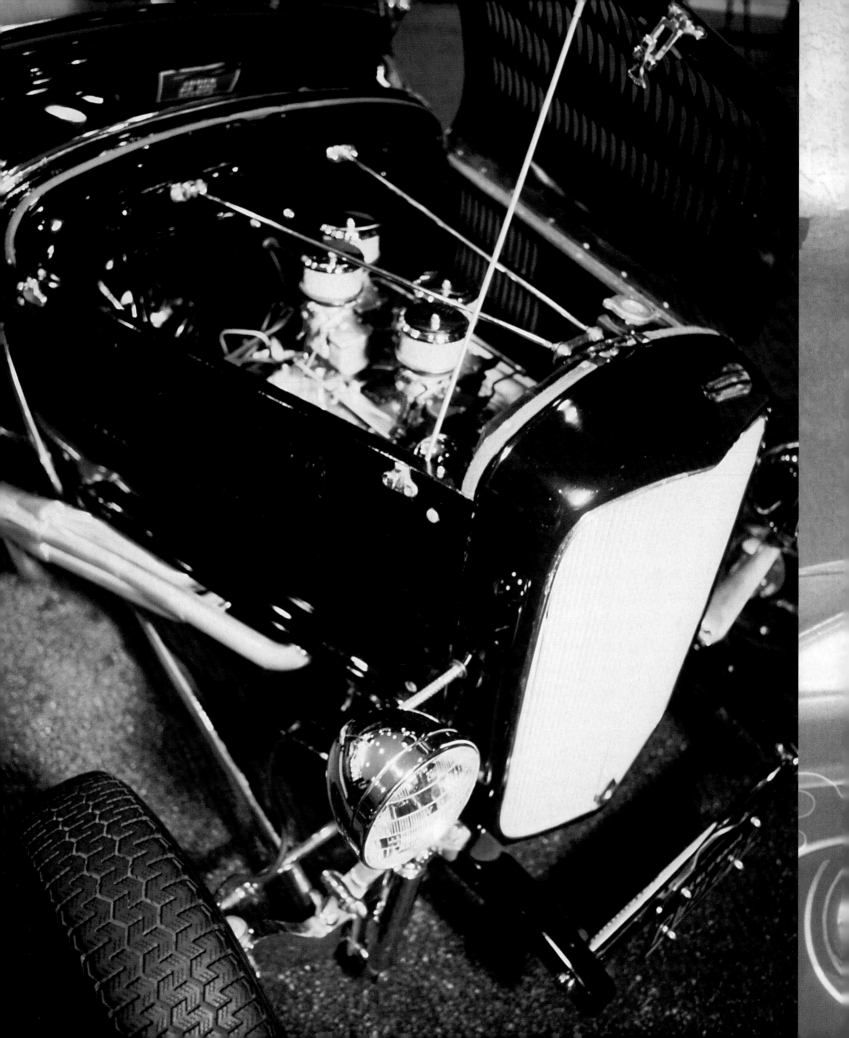

(Above and left) The 1932 Hi-Boy Roadster's original Ford motor was replaced with a high-compression Oldsmobile engine fitted with over-the-counter speed equipment. While not as glamorous and popular as the old Ford engine, the Oldsmobile was a logical choice because its overhead valve system provided horsepower that few Ford flatheads could match.
A customized 1965 Chevy Impala (below) beckons passers-by in Los Angeles.

FOR SALE

YEAR 65
MODEL Chevy Impala SS 327 Engine, Runs Good Front & Back Hydraulics!
PHONE $4500.00

(Top left, inset) A 1950 Mercury is in the radical custom treatment stage. The top has been lowered several inches, chrome trim has been removed (although the holes have not yet been filled), and the window frames have been raked back. Lead has been used to fill the body seams and fade the body's side character into one continuous contour. Custom cars were often called "lead sleds" because of the extensive use of this soft metal to create new body lines.

A 1948 Buick (above and bottom right, inset) displays the best of two worlds: elegant, original styling combined with a custom chrome grille. (Both cars, Collection of the Natural History Museum of Los Angeles County)

220 • AMERICA ON WHEELS

Hot rods are meant for racing and cruising, and from Atlantic City to Ft. Lauderdale to Los Angeles, people and their cars took to the streets. One place the phenomenon is archived is in the late 60s film, Hot Rods from Hell *(below)*.

*M*uscle cars, such as the 1967 Yenko-Chevrolet Camaro (below), continue to be some of the most coveted—and most consistently driven—collector's cars on the market.

THUNDERBIRD
ALWAYS GAVE YOU
THE MOON AND THE STARS...

FOR 1969
THUNDERBIRD GIVES YOU
THE SUN.

Take a new way to the sun: push the button opening Thunderbird's optional sliding sunroof. Go the Bird's way of long, low exterior design, interior décor to match every shade of opinion about luxury, power to answer all demands. Among personal-luxury cars only the Bird offers a choice of rooflines, body styles and seating arrangements. Go Thunderbird for all this. And heaven, too.

1969 Thunderbird 2-door Landau.

THUNDERBIRD Ford

the Corvair. It had different handling characteristics from other American cars because it was rear-engined and, therefore, had a rear weight bias. You had to be a little bit careful of it on icy or slippery roads. Europeans never had any problem with the Corvair because they were driving millions of Volkswagen Beetles which behaved exactly the same way on snow and ice.

"I think the Corvair controversy was perhaps the first, but by no means the last, example of when the public safety advocates, acting in close harmony with the trial lawyers—which is a pattern that's been richly established in later cases—where they blow some issue up to get the public steamed, and the networks, and the trial lawyers move in. And many of these consumer advocates then appear as expert witnesses."

(Above) Fred P. Duesenberg, son and nephew of the original Duesenberg Car Company brothers (1920-37), points to one of the two fuel tanks in his '60s version of the famous "Duesy." Innovations such as these did little to prevent this second incarnation from also folding.

Interestingly enough, by the time Nader's book was published, the Corvair's suspension problems had been corrected. GM still took a beating, though. And the company's response—hiring a private investigator in an attempt to dig up "dirt" on Nader—only fanned the flames of controversy.

"In November of 1965, having left the corporation several months earlier to join the University of Michigan, I had lunch with the assistant to the general counsel at GM, and she told me that there was no need to worry about that book because Ralph Nader was going to be discredited," says David Lewis. "I asked, 'How can that be?' And I was told, 'Well, we have ways to do that.' Subsequently I found out about those ways. General Motors tried to imply that Ralph Nader

was gay. It also tried to make him out as anti-semitic, inasmuch as he was of Lebanese descent."

GM's investigation did not simply fail; it back-fired. The company had seriously miscalculated both public response and Ralph Nader's resolve.

"GM treated him not as a new scholar of safety of the auto industry, but rather as an enemy, the way you would treat a foreign agent or traitor," says Harley Shaiken. "And I think what happened was a humbling of GM in very unexpected ways because that didn't sit well with people. GM's response seemed to be below the belt, unpatriotic in its own way. It showed a dimension of GM that I think GM deeply regretted in years subsequent to that incident."

In the end, Nader was awarded $425,000 in a settlement of his invasion-of-privacy suit against General Motors. Moreover, GM president James M. Roche publicly apologized to Nader before a Senate committee.

"Without delving into the accuracy of the book, which I think was largely nonexistent," says Robert Lutz, "I would admit that it did start the debate on automotive safety, which was needed."

Indeed, the legacy of the Corvair (GM ceased its production in 1969) is that it helped inspire the National Traffic and Motor Vehicle Safety Act, which in 1966 mandated seat belts and other improvements in passenger safety.

Federal regulation of the automobile industry was about to become a fact of life, and Detroit would never be the same. Big Brother was now riding in the backseat, looking over the Big Three's shoulder.

CHAPTER 9

Trouble in Paradise

In 1948 the number of automobiles manufactured in the United States reached the 100 million mark; just 15 years later, the figure was 200 million. And yet, despite this extraordinary growth, by the middle of the 1960s it was apparent that Detroit was under siege. Over the next two decades the increasingly imperious U.S. auto industry, blinded by its own record of success, would endure hardship on a grand scale. It would lose customers by failing to recognize sweeping changes in the global automobile market; and it would lose credibility by failing to manufacture products of uniformly high quality.

Eventually, in the late 1980s and early 1990s, the Big Three would rise spectacularly from the ashes. But the journey would be long and painful.

"I think there was a period of time in the postwar period

In the 1970s, the allegiance of the U.S. marketplace shifted to smaller, more reliable, high-mileage foreign imports; more than one million imports were registered by 1969. While American auto makers were slow to respond, certain domestic favorites like the muscular 1970 Mustang (right) still continued to sell.

when there was an arrogance with respect to, well, Detroit knows best, we know the answers to everything," says former Ford chief executive officer Philip Caldwell. "There has been some criticism of that, and I believe some of it was warranted. It doesn't matter whether it's automobiles or anything else—your customers should never be taken for granted. You're only there to serve your customers. You're not there to dominate your customers, to tell them what they need and all of that sort of thing."

Two unrelated events in 1955 foreshadowed problems for the industry. The first was the retirement of Alfred P. Sloan at General Motors. Without Sloan at the helm, GM lost much of the elasticity that had made it so successful; a company that had risen to greatness on a philosophy of flexibility suddenly found itself unable to adapt.

The second notable occurrence was the emergence of the foreign import—in the form of the Volkswagen Beetle—as a legitimate force in the automobile wars. The Beetle was invented in Germany in the 1930s and vigorously backed by Hitler, who called it the "Strength Through Joy" car. An admirer of Henry Ford, Hitler hoped to see the Beetle achieve the same degree of popularity in his country that the Model T had once enjoyed in the United States.

The Beetle was introduced to the U.S. market in 1949, but only two were sold that year. Six years later, with its Aryan roots sufficiently blurred, more than 20,000 were imported. By 1965 annual sales of

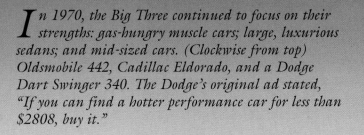

In 1970, the Big Three continued to focus on their strengths: gas-hungry muscle cars; large, luxurious sedans; and mid-sized cars. (Clockwise from top) Oldsmobile 442, Cadillac Eldorado, and a Dodge Dart Swinger 340. The Dodge's original ad stated, "If you can find a hotter performance car for less than $2808, buy it."

Everything we did about Volkswagen always brought you a smile, and it was almost by nature, we couldn't help ourselves. Even today, when somebody brings up the Bug, the Beetle, the VW, a smile comes to their faces. I don't know how many products in the history of time evoke that kind of response. It just left people with this wonderful affectionate feeling.

The fact that it was counterculture really appealed to me because I was in my early twenties then, and *I* was counterculture. I represented a new way of looking at things. And I loved the whole idea of doing things differently than the norm. And I think everybody who worked on Volkswagen was like that.

I don't know if we really were deep sociological or psychological thinkers. We just were doing what came naturally.

We used to say when they (the Big Three) zig we zag. And it was a conscious effort because we knew whatever they were doing was wrong. And we knew they weren't really talking to people. And we knew that's what we wanted to do. And we also wanted to get people to smile when we talked to them. So it was really a conscious effort to communicate on a different level.

I remember a 1969 VW ad that responded to Detroit's annual new car ads, longer, lower, wider, you know. And we had nothing new. So it seemed like a funny idea to say very quietly Volkswagen doesn't do it again. We didn't change it.

This is how the copy read: "Beautiful. It's not any longer. It's not any lower and it's not any wider. I can't believe it. The 1969 Volkswagen, 13 improvements, ugly as ever. Beautiful, just beautiful."

What were we doing? Thumbing our nose at what Detroit was doing.

Roy Grace
Advertising copywriter

230 • AMERICA ON WHEELS

the "Bug" reached 500,000 in the U.S., spear-heading a minimalist consumer movement. A particular favorite among hippies and college professors, the Beetle became a symbol of the counterculture in the late 1960s. It was a car whose popularity was closely linked to its very lack of styling and pre-tense. This was a vehicle designed to get the driver from point A to point B. Nothing more.

Of course, the irony is that this made the Beetle as much of a fashion statement as any car coming out of Detroit at the time. Advertising and marketing campaigns were self-deprecating and witty. But they also trumpeted the Beetle's attributes: namely, price.

"The underlying theme was, boy, you've got to be pretty stupid if you don't buy a Volkswagen," remembers Roy Grace, a New York advertising executive who did work for Volkswagen in the 1960s. "I mean, we didn't have strategies in those days. We just did what we thought was right. And the theme was, you can buy an American car for $3,000, or you can buy a Volkswagen and a washer and a dryer and a couple of television sets and a phonograph. So, who's the smart person now?

"It was a takeoff on 'Keeping up with the Joneses.' Everybody tries to keep up with their neighbors by obviously purchasing what they purchased. But this, I think, psychologically, was truly disarming to people because it said, 'Dummy, who's really keeping up with whom?'"

The Volkswagen was the antithesis of the American automobile. It was small, noisy, homely,

This station wagon seats 8. Sometimes.

and uncomfortable. But it was also functional, efficient, and economical. To those motorists annoyed by the concept of planned obsolescence, it was a welcome relief. The Beetle never changed. Year after year it looked the same, felt the same, sounded the same. To a large segment of the population, buying a Beetle was an effective way to make a statement; it was a way to rebel against the materialism and mass consumerism that had shaped American society in the postwar era.

"I owned a VW Bug, a used one, in the 1970s," says Ron Edsforth. "And the appealing part was that it was not an American car, and it was not a car that was trying to make some statement about my class aspirations. I was a graduate student at the time, and this car said that I was content to be what I was and scrape by on the income I had. At least that's what I felt."

The Volkswagen caught Americans, and the American automobile industry, completely off guard. It was generally accepted in the 1950s that there was no market for a small, essentially unattractive car whose only function was to provide basic transportation. But then along came the Beetle, forcing Detroit into a bit of reluctant self-examination.

The Big Three responded with small cars of their own, but the battle had really only just begun. By the end of the 1950s imported cars held a 10 percent share of the market, and by 1969 more than one million imports were registered in the United States. Half of these were Volkswagens. In 1973 sales of the Beetle passed the 15 million mark; the Little Car That Could was officially the most popular model ever sold in the United States, surpassing even Ford's legendary Model T. Quite an impressive achievement for a car once referred to by Henry Ford II as "a little shit box."

Competition from foreign car manufacturers was just one of the problems threatening Detroit's oligopoly in the late 1960s. Mounting concern over automobile safety and air pollution resulted in governmental intervention the likes of which the industry had never before known.

In the late 1950s a chemist working at the California Institute of Technology had become fascinated and appalled by the smog that was enveloping the city of Los Angeles. Arie Jan Haagen-Smit analyzed the contaminants in the air and discovered that they were strikingly similar to the elements found in automobile emissions. Haagen-Smit's conclusion, of course, was that the car was chiefly responsible for Los Angeles' air pollution problem, and, consequently, for a host of physiological problems afflicting the residents of Southern California.

Not surprisingly, the work of Haagen-Smit, and others like him, was quickly dismissed by the Big Three. There was, after all, no money to be made in the development and production of pollution-control devices. Worse, by acknowledging that the car was a major source of potentially dangerous pollutants, the industry would be stamping its own product with a "buyer beware" label. This was not exactly good for business.

Soon, though, Congress forced the issue. In 1965 the Vehicle Air Pollution and Control Act was passed. Tighter emissions standards were adopted, and automakers, in order to meet those standards, were compelled to make dramatic changes in the way they manufactured their products. But that was only the beginning. In 1970,

with the intensely ambitious Clean Air Act, Detroit was ordered to comply with legislation designed to reduce auto emissions by 90 percent over the next six years. Big Three executives tried to fight the legislation by arguing that current technology made the goal unattainable. Nevertheless, it went into effect.

"Not until 1965 did the government ask the industry to really try to lessen the social costs of its impact on the country," says Ron Edsforth. "And the industry had grown up not expecting that. Like most American industries, the auto industry assumes the role of government is to promote business, to subsidize the growth of their

(Left) Los Angeles, January 24, 1950, after a rainstorm. (Right) Los Angeles, October 14, 1950, "a nauseous blanket of smog cut visibility to less than two city blocks and caused Gov. Goodwin J. Knight to…see what action he can take…to help alleviate the sickening siege…." (AP-Wire photo)

corporation, their industry. Not to get in the way of its growth. Because, after all, if you tell the company to make a more safe car, a less polluting car, you're intruding on its right to design the car freely, to engineer it, to produce it—to price it even, because you are probably adding to the cost of the car."

True enough. But by the mid-1970s, anti-pollution efforts—which included the introduction of unleaded gasoline and the catalytic converter—were paying off. Despite continued growth in the automobile population, air pollution directly attributable to auto emissions began to drop.

Consumer advocacy groups in the 1970s also continued their campaign for safer automobiles.

Control and balance make it a beautiful experience.

Most people look at waves and just see water. To them, a road's just pavement. But if you think there's more to life, we've got something for you.

Mustang's new Sprint Decor Option. Sporty colors inside and out. Dual racing mirrors that look right at home.

Even the interior of the Sprint Decor Option is a new experience. A panoramic instrument panel and a floor-mounted stick shift sitting between bucket seats. Now this is the real way to control a car.

Its stabilizer bar and independent front suspension help give you a more balanced ride. Around curves and over bumps.

The Sprint Decor Option is available in the Hardtop and SportsRoof models. Mag wheels, raised white letter tires and competition suspension are also available.

1972 Ford Mustang SportsRoof shown with Sprint Decor Option.

FORD MUSTANG

FORD DIVISION *Ford*

1972 Ford Mustang Hardtop shown with Sprint Decor Option.

Seat belts, padded dashboards, and improved braking systems all became commonplace. So, too, did recalls of cars deemed unsafe for highway travel. In order to correct defects that prevented automobiles from meeting the new federally mandated safety standards, more than 10 million automobiles were recalled between 1965 and 1975. All of this, naturally, led to increased car prices—an average of $300 per vehicle by 1974. Nevertheless, Detroit kept pumping out record numbers of cars...big cars, mostly.

Despite the impressive performance of the Volkswagen and other small foreign imports, U.S. automobile manufacturers continued to view the

In 1973 the typical domestic automobile averaged less than 15 miles per gallon. Gas-guzzling cars became positively gluttonous with the advent of antipollution devices and air conditioning, both of which reduced fuel efficiency. This might have been tolerated with little more than a shrug if not for a sudden shortage of gasoline in the fall of 1973, when the oil-rich countries of the Middle East declared an embargo against Israel and its allies, including the United States.

For many motorists the oil embargo was frightening and infuriating. Accustomed to filling up whenever and wherever they wanted, drivers were now forced to wait in long lines. And when they

Despite a mediocre mechanical record and average to poor fuel efficiency, certain American models were mainstays in the car market: the sporty Corvette (above and right) and stylish Cadillac (top right) were and still are quite popularly traded American cars.

compact car as a risky investment. The profit margin was simply too slim. In 1969, even as the Beetle was taking the country by storm—and even as the Big Three were introducing compacts of their own—large and midsize cars still held a commanding 72 percent share of the U.S. market. Clearly this indicated a reluctance on the part of most American consumers to relinquish their inalienable right to sit high above the highway; they wanted cars, not...*toys*. Soon, however, circumstances would dictate sweeping changes in consumer attitudes and buying patterns.

finally reached the pump, they often discovered not only skyrocketing prices, but also a ceiling on how much they were allowed to purchase. Moreover, a nationwide 55-mph speed limit was imposed to help conserve gasoline. Not since World War II had the United States experienced anything like it.

"I had a family, I had children, and I needed transportation, lots of room, all kinds of garbage that I had to take with me," remembers Roy Grace. "So I bought the world's largest station wagon. Really, to this day, it seems like a building to me rather than a car. It was huge. It was a

Mercury Marquis. I think it was the biggest station wagon sold at the time. And I think I had it about two weeks when the first energy crisis struck. I remember queuing up on my first line around the block to try and fill up this tank, and getting finally to my spot in the line and I could only buy $2 worth of gas, which was essentially a thimblefull for this car. I had that car a very short time. I unloaded it very, very quickly. It was impractical, totally. Especially in the world of no gas."

As it turned out, the crisis lasted just six months. And even in that time there was no "real" shortage. Later it would be revealed that thou-

In October, 1973, after the outbreak of an Arab-Israeli war, Arabic countries declared an embargo on oil to Israel and its allies—including the United States. This resulted in huge lines at gas stations, rationing, and outlandish prices. While this complicated situation was resolved within six months, questions still linger about the oil industry's byzantine system of price regulation.

sands of barrels of Arab oil were somehow reaching the U.S. each day. The crude, however, wasn't making its way to the consumer; rather, it was stockpiled. Whether this was a precautionary measure taken by the government or a calculated attempt by the oil companies to inflate prices became a point of considerable debate. Regardless of the motive, however, the effect was devastating. American motorists began demanding smaller, more efficient cars. And if Detroit couldn't produce them, the consumer would turn to the imports.

The Big Three were manufacturing small cars in the early 1970s, of course. Unfortunately, they weren't making enough of them, and they weren't making them very well. Among the new breed of "subcompacts" were the Ford Pinto and the Chevrolet Vega, both of which were public relations nightmares.

The Vega was simply a car prone to mechanical failure of one sort or another. In 1971, in an attempt to increase the Vega's profitability, General Motors had dramatically cut labor costs through the use of automation. Each hour, more than 100 Vegas rolled off Chevrolet's Lordstown, Ohio, assembly line—a 67 percent increase in productivity from the previous year. There was a steep cost, though. In 1972 workers at the Lordstown facility, exhausted by the back-breaking pace required to keep up with the robots on the assembly line, went out on strike.

GM management negotiated a settlement with the union essentially by agreeing to run the plant with a lighter touch. Still, the point had been made: assembly line work, while not as brutal as it was in the 1930s, was still difficult, depressing work. And despite the high wages and benefits that came with unionization, employees were often beaten into apathy or negligence.

"Life in the factory was very lucrative in that you made a lot of money," says Sam Kirkland, a UAW representative who has worked in the auto industry for nearly two decades. "And it was also so fast that you felt like you were being pushed to put out the product and nobody seemed to ask

As the Big Three attempted to catch up to the quality of the Japanese and the quantity of subcompact cars, the trial and error would catch up with them. Quality control was undervalued, and cars like the Vega (above) were symbolic of the problem; the Vega was recalled three separate times for safety infractions, and it also had a notoriously high rate of mechanical problems.

you, you know, could this be done better? Mostly the question at that point was, could we do more of it? Could we do it faster?"

With an increase in quantity came a decrease in quality. The Vega became one of the most notoriously unreliable cars of the 1970s. Three times it was recalled because of safety defects. And owners often found themselves bringing the car back for engine and brake repairs. The Vega became a symbol of Detroit's inability to make a quality car for the subcompact market.

The story of the Pinto, meanwhile, was far more disturbing. The car was the subject of several lawsuits in the 1970s. In one, a California jury awarded damages of $128 million after an accident in which a driver was killed and a passenger severely burned when their Pinto was rear-ended on a Los Angeles freeway and burst into flames. In another case, three young people were killed when their Pinto exploded after being rear-ended. Ford subsequently became the first car company in U.S. history to be charged with criminal homicide. Ford was ultimately exonerated, but not before a lengthy and well-publicized trial had done considerable damage to the company's reputation.

"In the Sixties and early Seventies, and even the late Seventies, there was a huge quality prob-

lem in American industry," says Robert Lutz. "It wasn't just the car business. TV sets broke down, washing machines broke down—everything we made and sold to each other was prone to a lot of defects. And I think it was, in a sense, complacency. We were the biggest country, the richest country, militarily the most important country. And we didn't see the need for continuous improvement because...we're great, we're number one. Who's to challenge us?

"You still see it in the service industry, the same attitude that we used to have, which is, it's good enough. I mean, people are buying it. You know, they're coming to the restaurant. What's to complain about? So, okay, every now and then somebody has a glass with a little lipstick on it. So what? We'll give them another. It's that attitude of, we've got plenty of customers, what the heck's the problem? The few who complain? We'll take care of them. But we must be doing all right because look at all the people. People are still coming. It was that sort of attitude: *We're doing good enough.* And, in fact, we weren't."

In November of 1979 the American motorist and the American automobile industry once again felt the sting of a gasoline shortage. This crisis began when United States embassy personnel in

The Pinto (left) was another poorly executed American subcompact car, and several even blew up when they were rear-ended. Several lawsuits resulted, and it is generally considered one of the low points in the history of American auto making. There were, of course, some high points: the niche market for utility vehicles, like the Chevy El Camino (top right), Jeeps, and the ever-popular pick-up trucks (Chevrolets at middle and bottom right) provided a steady demand for certain American cars throughout the 1970s to the present.

'77 CHEVY TRUCKS.
TOUGH IN THE RIGHT PLACES.

Iran were taken hostage. The U.S. responded, in part, by placing an embargo on Iranian oil. For the second time in less than a decade there were long lines and high prices at the gas pump.

"The 1979 oil price shock is really the determining shock that shakes up the industry and forces them to adjust some of their thinking about what kind of cars they make and the way they produce them," says Ron Edsforth. "It confirms the direction of the market in the 1970s. It makes clear that the imported cars are here to stay, that the foreign manufacturers are here to stay. In fact, the foreign manufacturers are making plans to build plants in the United States by that point in time."

The Big Three recognized too late the threat to their dominance. And, even once awakened, they were ill-equipped to respond. Over the course of the next five years motorists would vote, as they always had, with their checkbooks. The clear winner would be Japan; the loser, Detroit.

"Until the latter part of the Seventies, Americans didn't want to be crammed into the smaller space of the smaller cars," says Philip Caldwell. "But the thing that really made the

difference was the second fuel crisis. People could see that fuel lines were beginning to form in certain parts of the country, and they were scared to death that they weren't going to be able to use their motorcar. So all of a sudden, the Japanese just started pouring their cars into the United States. And people started buying them because, they said, compared to no car, no transportation, it's better to have a small car with small gasoline requirements. And that's how it really got a big toehold."

In truth, Japanese automakers had been improving their position within the marketplace for years; their products did not suddenly appear on showroom floors in 1978, beckoning angst-ridden drivers who no longer felt any affection for big, thirsty American-made cars. But once American motorists began buying Hondas and Nissans and Toyotas—once they discovered that these cars were not only fuel efficient, but mechanically sound as well—they fell in love.

Ironically, the words "Made in Japan," once a derisive stamp emblematic of nothing so much as shoddy craftsmanship, now came to represent

Japanese cars like this affordable little 1978 Honda Civic proved to be highly reliable and fuel efficient, and with another gas price surge in 1979, Americans started to find these cars quite desirable—despite the fact that their aesthetics and performance didn't measure up to many American cars.

excellence. Japanese products, in a relatively few short years, eclipsed American products in the eyes of the consumer. Confidence in Japanese cars began to rise dramatically. Through a combination of advertising and word of mouth, the message came through: *It's time for a change.* Indeed, by 1980, Japan had replaced the United States as the leading automobile manufacturer in the world.

"A lot of events started to coalesce at one time," says Philip Caldwell. "So the landscape looked something like this in the latter part of the Seventies: You had the fuel economy problem staring everybody in the face because of the prospective reduction in the available gasoline; you had the quality problem; you had the cost problem from the yen-dollar relationship. At the same time, there was this great envelope of regulations overshadowing everybody. The regulations had timetables that said you have to have this safety factor in by a certain date. You have to have this emission achievement by a certain date. We had conflicting priorities, and they were all coming together at one time.

"Now, the *coup de grace* to all of this is, starting in 1980 and '81 and '82—the greatest recession-slash-depression for the auto industry since the mid-Thirties. Those were the days when the clouds were pretty dark. There weren't many sunny days for anybody."

Except for the Japanese and European car makers, of course. For them, life was wonderful. And deservedly so. If the lure of economy and efficiency first brought U.S. consumers to Honda and Toyota showrooms, quality brought them back. At the same time, the Big Three were suffering from an embarrassment of glitches. By 1977 Detroit was recalling as many cars as it sold; by 1980 industry observers estimated that for every 100 American cars coming off the assembly line, there were 700 defects.

"The Japanese in the 1970s and '80s accus-

At first they were like sewing machines. They were very awkward little cars. But I didn't ever think of the Japanese imports, even in the early phases, as a joke. But I did not see them as great examples of design, or even good examples of design. I didn't see them as a threat. I really didn't. And I thought, well, they're going to take an awful long time to catch up design-wise. But they didn't. They changed and they continued to change until they started to get it right.

The big plus they had going for them when they became successful is that they were small cars which addressed the fuel economy issues that everybody was concerned about at the time. So they just happened to be at the right place at the right time and it seemed to click for them.

Jack Telnack
Automotive designer

tomed Americans to an entirely different quality standard," says Robert Lutz. "The defect-free standard; the vehicle that almost never has to go back to the dealer for a repair."

Interestingly enough, the Japanese learned the finer points of mass production from their U.S. counterparts. Soichiro Honda was an eight-year-old boy in the small village of Hamamatsu when he saw an automobile for the first time. The sight of that Model T had a profound impact on Honda; in fact, it was the moment "when I dreamed of manufacturing a car myself some day," he would later say. (Half a century later he offered to sell a half-interest in his budding company to Ford, but Henry Ford II, seeing no benefit to such a partnership, turned him down.)

Honda was one of many Japanese industrial leaders who looked to the U.S. as a source of inspi-

Honda sent a real warrior over in the 1978 Accord, one of the first subcompact Japanese cars to feature great styling. The combination of looks, performance, price, and mechanical excellence made this one of the best—and, by 1989, the best—selling cars in America. The quality control and the absolute dedication of the Japanese worker was to be a great inspiration to American auto companies and led to the eventual resurgence of the American automobile.

ration after the devastation of World War II. Japanese automakers visited American plants (for example, Eiji Toyoda, a member of Toyota's founding family, worked at the River Rouge for several months in the early 1950s). They absorbed the technology and then adapted it to fit their own society. They created massive factories where work was broken down into specific operations to be carried out by teams working together. This was fundamentally different from the American approach to mass production. In U.S. industry there often existed a deep hostility between supervisor and worker; in Japan, there was not only mutual respect, but constant dialogue. Management valued the input of the assembly-line worker because he was closest to the production process.

In their efforts, the Japanese were helped by American efficiency experts who had found little support for their ideas at home.

"The Japanese, in their manufacturing excellence, in the 1960s, '70s, and '80s, where they had a clear lead over us, they didn't really invent anything," says Robert Lutz. "They used many of the techniques that we ourselves had developed in the Twenties, Thirties, and Forties. The Japanese simply applied sound Western-developed manufacturing discipline and applied it unwaveringly and with absolute discipline. And what happened with us is we lost the discipline. It was as simple as that."

Far more complicated than the diagnosis was the cure. By the early 1980s U.S. automakers had no choice but to swallow their pride and admit that they not only had serious problems but that there was also much they could learn from their Japanese and European counterparts.

For the Big Three, it was time to go back to school.

Honda wasn't the only Japanese export making waves in America; the Toyota Corolla outsold many domestic cars as a result of its superior workmanship and economy.

"Madeen" Japan: When I was a kid I thought it was a town. Made in Japan meant junk. The worst little tinny pieces of crap you bought. Candy store stuff. Little tin and plastic pieces of nonsense.

By the late '70s an enormous and dynamic shift occurred, not only in the perception of the American public, but in the reality of the product. Americans had become complacent and were turning out shoddy products, or certainly not top quality.

The Japanese were making far better products. And Americans were buying the best quality they could find. Consumers were making the smart purchase.

When I first met with Mr. Eiji Toyoda, he surprised me by telling me that he personally had spent three months or so in Ford's Rouge plant, about 1950. He came to look at it to see how it worked. He was employed in the plant, as I understand what he was telling me, and he saw it (working).

Then he went back to Japan and put what he'd learned into effect there. And he had very great respect and, I think, a feeling of gratitude about it, really, as strange as that might seem to some people. There was respect for the concept, there was a respect for the execution. There was a respect for the output of the whole thing because this was the way that you got low cost. And low costs were reflected in low prices and low prices meant many people could enjoy the mobility, which is what a motor vehicle really provides.

That was the whole idea and he had always thought of building his car for many people, not just a few people. And that was his whole idea in life.

Philip Caldwell
Former CEO, Ford Motor Co.

CHAPTER 10

The Empire Strikes Back

In October of 1979 Philip Caldwell became the first person outside the Ford family to be named chief executive officer of the Ford Motor Company. At the end of his first day on the job, Caldwell walked out of his office, stepped onto an elevator, and found himself sharing a ride with his predecessor, Henry Ford II.

This was a bad time for the Ford Motor Company, of course, just as it was a bad time for the entire U.S. automobile industry. Caldwell inherited the helm of a company still reeling from the ugliness of the Pinto disaster; a company desperately trying to survive the Japanese invasion. The two men rode quietly. Finally, Hank the Deuce, who knew a little something about guiding a damaged ship through turbulent waters, broke the silence.

A dramatic comeback was in the making as the Big Three combined a rededication to quality, hard lessons learned from the Japanese (including downsizing and increased automation), some European design flavor, and American ingenuity to again produce top-notch American cars—like the Dodge Stealth (left).

The Honda Accord continued to be a benchmark vehicle in the 1980s. As Detroit would learn, many Americans—including the crucial "baby boomer" market—became quite accustomed to the quality of these Japanese cars. To make matters worse, in 1982 Honda opened a plant in Ohio—with American workers—and continued to produce an abundance of highly-acclaimed cars.

"I'm really sorry to leave you with all this mess," he said.

Caldwell smiled. "Well, my recollection is that when you took over, you had a lot of problems, too. You had severe problems, deeper than the ones we're talking about now."

True enough, Ford said. But there was a difference. A major difference.

"I had one thing going for me," Ford said. "We could sell anything we built. You can't, because people don't *have* to buy our cars now. There are lots of cars out there that they can buy; lots of good cars."

Indeed there were. Unfortunately, very few of them were being produced in Detroit. At their peak, the Japanese automakers would own a 28 percent share of the U.S. market. A massive chunk for a foreign competitor, to be sure, but even more impressive than the sales figures was the gut-level response to the imports. In 1986, for example, Honda was fourth in U.S. sales, but first in customer satisfaction.

Meanwhile, the Big Three stumbled along, spilling red ink all over their ledgers. In the early 1980s Chrysler lost as much as $1.7 billion in a single year; Ford lost $1.5 billion and General Motors $763 million. By this time all three corporations were taking a long, hard look in the mirror and coming to the stark realization that they were in fact producing inferior automobiles. Atonement, they knew, was the first step on the road to redemption.

"There was a turning point in there, some time in the early Eighties, where it was accepted that we had to raise our quality and our productivity, the standard of excellence of everything that we do, or we weren't going to make it in business," says Ford Motor Company chief executive officer Alexander Trotman.

"At Ford, there was a commitment to work together as a team to make ourselves much more competitive. I think that was a major turning point in relationships between all of us—among the management and the union leadership and the hourly work force, the salaried work force."

Of the Big Three, only Chrysler was legitimately on the cusp of ruination in the early 1980s. Ford and General Motors had the resources to survive almost anything. Still, there is no denying that for each of the industry giants, this was an extremely difficult period. Not since the Great Depression had they faced such a challenge. Ironically, that record of success was now a liability, rather than an asset, for Detroit was suffering from a distinct lack of institutional memory: No one working in upper management at the Big Three had any first-hand experience with this sort of economic crisis; life had been too good for too long. In engineering a comeback, U.S. automakers had to rely on nothing so much as common sense.

"When you have a hard time selling the products you're selling because they don't have quality, and you know that they don't have quality, you don't have to be told that forever," says Philip Caldwell. "Pretty soon you get the message. And so the question becomes, what are you going to do about it? How will you get something done about it? At Ford, it was pretty clear that there was one thing we could do. And that was, instead of having the poorest quality—which we did among the Big Three at the beginning—we could have the best.

"Everybody was perfectly willing to get on board. Our people were loyal and

The Big Three were learning their lesson: in the early 1980s models like the Chevy Cavalier (top) and the Ford Escort (bottom) competed successfully in the subcompact market. With quality steadily improving, these unspectacular but capable cars were priced right and performed well. Both were able to place in the top ten in U.S. sales into the 1990s.

competent and committed. We needed to build better products. So we decided that we were going to make quality the number one goal of the Ford Motor Company. Of all the goals out there, that was going to be our number one objective. And we've lived by that ever since. That was legitimate. That was fundamental. And we got it done."

Eventually, yes. But not before losing $1.5 billion in 1980, $1.1 billion in 1981, and $700 million in 1982—$3.3 billion in three years, an astounding figure for a company that had not reported an annual loss since World War II.

"Quality isn't something you can buy at the grocery store," Caldwell says. "It's something you have to earn, piece by piece, step by step, day by day, dollar by dollar spent. That takes a long time. This is real slow-release fertilizer, and it's a long time before the grass becomes green. In our case it took two years of serious dedication before we could see any achievement at all. And we wondered many times, what are we missing? But we kept on turning over every single rock, looking at every facet of the business."

More than anything else, Ford was motivated by desperation.

"It's a very big task. I mean, if you've been pushing against the door for a few hours, pretty soon you begin to say, 'Well, I guess there's no way I can get the door open,'" Caldwell says. "But the idea is, you *have* to get to the other side. And the only way you can get to the other side is through that door. That's the situation we were in."

The life of a big three automotive executive is so cosseted, is so incestuous, is so imperial in its trappings and purposes, it is so insulated from contact with the sordid, with the uncomfortable, or with the consumer. They get a new car every three months. They are driven to work by chauffeurs. Their cars are daily maintained and inspected. They have never had to buy a car at a dealership. They have never had to cope with an automotive salesman. They have never had to wait for repairs.

And what happens to imperially treated people is that they become isolated, arrogant, and imperial. It is extremely hard not to.

Laurel Cutler
Automobile executive

As the 1970s gave way to the 1980s, Ford had a profitable and respected line of trucks. Among car owners, however, the company had become something of a joke. It was fine that this issue had been addressed, and Ford had made a decision to confront head-on the quality-control problems that had resulted in vehicles such as the Pinto. But that was not enough. Ford needed something completely different: a midsize car that would be striking in both design and performance.

That car was the Taurus. Conceived in 1980 and introduced in 1985, the Taurus (named after the astrological sign of the wife of one of the car's designers) was instrumental in reversing the fortunes of the Ford Motor Company. Its unique, aerodynamic styling (first introduced on the 1983 Thunderbird) was mockingly dubbed "the jellybean look" by critics and competitors. Consumers, though, loved the car's sleek appearance.

The Taurus was unveiled amid great pomp and circumstance in January, 1985, at the MGM sound stage in Culver City, California. The event served as both a coming-out party for the Taurus and a farewell tribute to Caldwell, who would soon be succeeded as Ford CEO by Don Petersen. Los Angeles public relations wizard Robert Janni, who had organized the spectacularly glitzy opening and closing ceremonies at the 1984 Summer Olympics, presided over the lavish Hollywood affair. It featured, appropriately enough, a science fiction motif, with automated waiters serving drinks to guests, and a stage that resembled a spaceship.

The party was a hit, but it wasn't until the Taurus reached showroom floors 11 months later that public response could be accurately gauged. To say the car was popular would be a gross understatement. Despite glitches that prompted the recall of 4,500 vehicles in the first week alone, the Taurus became an unqualified success. Dealers could not keep the car in stock. It helped, of course, that the Taurus performed well. Minor defects notwithstanding, it was a smooth, efficient car, at once economical, comfortable, and fun to drive. What really sparked interest in the Taurus, though, was its design. For the first time, an American automobile manufacturer had produced a car that did not look typically American. It was

1991 Ford Taurus

rounder, more stylish—with lines that begged comparison to pricier European models.

"Some of our competitors were very helpful to stir the pot of controversy with respect to the shape," Philip Caldwell says. "But that didn't last very long. I mean, they sort of questioned the wisdom of the shape. And as a matter of fact, it was even at one time called the hot dog because it looked sort of round and that sort of thing. But we knew that the shape could be a very distinguishing factor with respect to our car on the road. Everybody would say, 'Oh, there's the Taurus.' And that's exactly what happened. It influenced

our designs throughout the rest of our product line, and indeed it's influenced the designs of everybody's product line."

To its credit, Ford was unwavering in its dedication to the Taurus. Caldwell committed $3 billion to the project even as his company was reporting record losses. In the end, that faith and perseverance was handsomely rewarded. The Taurus was named *Motor Trend* Car of the Year in 1986, and it soon became the best-selling domestic car on the market, a position it would maintain for the better part of a decade.

The Ford Motor Company actually turned the corner in 1983, two years before the Taurus was introduced, when it posted record earnings of $1.9 billion. In 1984, as the U.S. emerged fully from a recession, Ford earned $2.9 billion, thanks in part to public response to the redesigned Thunderbird and the new Tempo. By 1986 profits had soared to $3.3 billion, nearly twice what arch-rival General Motors had posted (an incredible accomplishment considering GM was 40 percent larger than Ford). And that was merely a prelude.

The huge popularity of the Taurus, coupled with renewed interest in the company's high-end "Panther" cars (the Lincoln Continental, Lincoln Town Car, Ford Crown Victoria, and Mercury Grand Marquis) helped Ford earned $4.6 billion in 1987 and $5.3 billion in 1988. In 1989 Ford Motor Company stock hit an all-time high; not coincidentally, Don Petersen was named Man of the Year by *Motor Trend*. In 1990, the Lincoln Town Car was named *Motor Trend* Car of the Year. It was the fourth time in five years that a Ford product had been so honored.

Courage and ingenuity were only two factors in Ford's resurrection. Practicality entered into the equation, too. At the same time that it was devel-

We could not get to profitability until we could build larger-size cars. We had to build new larger-size cars because the market did not want to buy our old ones. And that was the groundwork for what became the Taurus.

In 1980, we decided to go ahead with the Taurus program...estimated to cost 3 billion dollars. In that year, we lost a billion and a half dollars. We didn't know we were going to lose a billion and a half...but we knew we were in a loss situation. We also didn't know we were going to lose 1.1 billion dollars in 1981, and we didn't know we were going to lose another 700 million dollars in 1982.

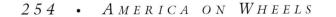

In all, 3.3 billion dollars for the whole company.

At the same time, we committed ourselves to spending 3 billion dollars to build the Taurus car line.

It was our finest hour because everybody in the company who had anything to do with it—the relevant people were quite a few—were fully committed to going ahead with this program. They did not know how it was going to turn out. They knew that everything had to work. What was the alternative? There was no alternative.

Philip Caldwell, Former CEO, Ford Motor Company

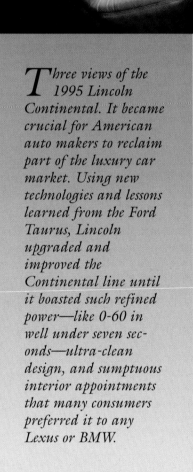

Three views of the 1995 Lincoln Continental. It became crucial for American auto makers to reclaim part of the luxury car market. Using new technologies and lessons learned from the Ford Taurus, Lincoln upgraded and improved the Continental line until it boasted such refined power—like 0-60 in well under seven seconds—ultra-clean design, and sumptuous interior appointments that many consumers preferred it to any Lexus or BMW.

oping the Taurus, Ford drastically reduced its work force. Over a period of six years—from 1979 to 1985—employment worldwide fell from 515,000 to 375,000; between 1979 and 1983, the hourly work force was trimmed from 191,000 to 101,000. And yet, with the help of automation and sound management, production levels remained essentially unchanged. In this way Ford reduced its annual operating cost by $5 billion.

It was, indisputably, good business. But there was a tremendous human toll to this fiscal redesign. Not just at Ford, but throughout the auto industry.

Once this competition really takes hold at the end of the 1970s, the Big Three close a lot of factories that were built as early as the 1920s," says Ron Edsforth. "Simply in order to bring things up to world standards they build new facilities with all new technology inside them—they couldn't just retool the old factories. As part of that process, machines were going to replace more human labor. And as a result, the industry's work force would shrink dramatically. That was one of the most basic steps they had to take. They had an excess capacity that they had to shed. And that is a difficult process. That is a wrenching process.

"By shutting factories, by building new factories, installing new technologies, at the same time cutting the work force by close to 50 percent, they are able to vastly increase productivity, which means they're able to produce as many cars now as they did years and years ago with far fewer workers. But who pays the price here? The person who pays the biggest price is the worker who loses his job or her job. That is gone forever for most of them. Those workers are shed from the industry and are in a much more insecure, uncertain economic environment."

Among the landmark events in Detroit's fall from grace was the opening of a Honda Motor Company plant in Marysville, Ohio, in November, 1982. Big Three executives, in their quest for a level playing field, had insisted that the Japanese begin manufacturing cars in the United States. In

No longer stuck with compromises when buying an American car, one could purchase a well-built domestic car that could be sporty or elegant, and high-performance. And between the Big Three, there emerged enough affordable choices—like the 1991 Ford Probe (below)—that consumers could express their individuality, which is central to the identity of the American consumer.

this way the Japanese would not be able to take advantage of a cheap, compliant labor force; rather, they would be strangled by an American work force that was sloppy, spoiled, and lazy. Just like the Big Three.

Or so went the conventional wisdom.

The plan, however, backfired. With American workers—albeit, non-unionized workers—manning the assembly lines, Honda began churning out Accords at a record pace. The cars were inex-

pensive, attractive, and well-built. Soon, the myth of the inept and arrogant American worker was exploded. Just one year later General Motors acknowledged the obvious—that it could learn a great deal about management, technology...even

marketing—from the Japanese. They entered into an agreement with Toyota to produce cars at a GM plant that had been shut down in Fremont, California.

"The Japanese became a tremendous danger and threat to Detroit," says Laurel Cutler. "Now, how did they do that? In the first place, they were the first people to market automotive products in this country. The customer had no role whatsoever in Detroit's planning. The customer came in at the end of a five-year process of development, and not a moment before. Honda understood what the young American wanted in a car."

By catering to the customer, and by manufacturing the best cars in the world, the Japanese were able to break a decades-old tradition of brand loyalty in the United States. Once, it was common for the first-time car buyer to purchase a Chevrolet (or a Ford or a Pontiac or a Buick) simply because that is what his father had bought. No longer. The motorist of the 1980s would not be hamstrung by sentiment; to him, all that mattered were price and quality.

What Detroit failed to recognize—until it was nearly too late—was the staggering influence of this new generation of consumers. These, after all, were the baby boomers. The yuppies.

"What was never really printed was the fact that boomers by and large had never bought an American car," says Laurel Cutler. It wasn't their parents who were buying the Japanese cars; it was the largest generation of car buyers who had never driven an American car and were being kept very happy and satisfied by the Japanese. Detroit had lost the boomer generation, and that was very frightening. When it finally was forced to their attention who these buyers were that they had lost—not just how many of them there were, but *who* they were—then they got busy. And they started matching the quality."

Chrysler's comeback was engineered by Lee Iacocca, one of the most charismatic and influential men Detroit has ever known. In the 1960s Iacocca had helped bring the Mustang to life at Ford. After a well-publicized falling out with Henry Ford II, however, he was dismissed from the company in 1978, but within a few months he was running the show at beleaguered Chrysler. In 1980 Chrysler was virtually broke, prompting an unsuccessful attempt by Iacocca to sell the company to Ford. If not for a $1.2 billion guaranteed

Lee Iacocca's (left) revolutionary success and the quality of the Ford Mustang, fueled his ascendancy to the chairmanship of both Ford and Chrysler. For a time, he was even mentioned as a potential U.S. presidential candidate. (Above, left) Sparring in the boardroom with one-time boss, Henry Ford II.

loan from the government—the largest federal bail-out in history—Chrysler might well have gone under.

As it happened, though, the company roared back. Like Ford, Chrysler got lean and mean in the early 1980s, slashing its work force—white-collar and blue-collar—nearly in half. In the first quarter of 1984, thanks in part to strong performances by its K-cars, Chrysler showed a profit of more than $700 million—a figure that exceeded the compa-

On its bumpy road to recovery, Chrysler found short-term rejuvenation under Lee Iacocca before unveiling a hugely successful line of cars; like the Chrysler Concorde and Eagle Vision, the 1995 Dodge Intrepid (below) is a highly regarded new breed of mid-size sedan.

General Motors may have been the last of the Big Three to reestablish its reputation, but J.D. Power & Associates rated four GM cars in its top ten in May 1995. (Clockwise from top) Its 1995 flagship Cadillac line: Seville, Deville Concours, and Eldorado.

What Mustang is to the Ford line, the Corvette is to Chevrolet. The former is in its fourth decade of production, and the latter is in its fifth. And while aficionados can argue amicably about the most glorious of these cars—be it the 1956 Corvette or the 1966 hardtop Mustang—the technological prowess of the 1995 Corvette (left and below) would surely garner plenty of votes.

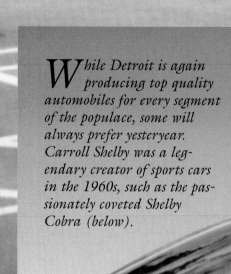

While Detroit is again producing top quality automobiles for every segment of the populace, some will always prefer yesteryear. Carroll Shelby was a legendary creator of sports cars in the 1960s, such as the passionately coveted Shelby Cobra (below).

The hardest part about coming back, and it's still the hardest part, is that we have to fight the perception issue. In other words—even though the reality of the superior Japanese automobile is for all intents and purposes gone—it's very hard to get many consumers back to even try an American car. For again very rational reasons. People say, well, I've had five Hondas or five Toyotas and I loved them. Why should I, why should I take the risk?

And our answer is, the reason you should try us is, and I mean any of the Big Three, the reason you should try us is we today build vehicles that are every bit as good and they're priced 2 to 3,000 dollars less. That's the rational reason why you should try us.

Robert Lutz
President, Chrysler Corporation

ny's prior record for profits in an entire *year*! By the end of 1984 Chrysler had made $2.38 billion; earnings for the following year were $1.64 billion.

It was a remarkable turnaround. Not surprisingly, the man who ran Chrysler became a celebrity. Iacocca's autobiography was an international best seller. He starred in Chrysler commercials; In one memorable 1981 spot, Iacocca brazenly challenged customers: "If you can find a better car, buy it." He appeared on the cover of *Time*, and even made a cameo appearance on an episode of "Miami Vice," one of the hottest television shows of its time. There was even talk that Iacocca might run for President of the United States. Of course, there would be problems down the road. Chrysler would stumble again in the late 1980s, and Iacocca—who had graciously accepted a salary of just one dollar when Chrysler was at its nadir, in 1980—would be severely criticized for paying himself more than $20 million in 1987. For now, though, life at Chrysler was positively euphoric.

Not so at General Motors, where a series of miscalculations, coupled with a

The 1996 Plymouth Neon coupe, an affordable and fun-to-drive member of America's new breed of cars.

stubbornness unmatched in the business, very nearly brought a giant to its knees.

GM made $4.5 billion in 1984 and owned 44 percent of the U.S. market. But there were huge cracks in the foundation. In terms of quality, GM cars were the worst of the Big Three (the company was spending nearly $2 billion annually on warranty claims). Moreover, GM remained, in many ways, the fattest of the auto manufacturers (throughout the 1980s, and even into the early 1990s, the average GM car required 35 hours of labor; Ford, by contrast, needed just 25 hours to build a car).

GM's joint venture with Toyota in California should have been a valuable learning experience, but it was not. The two companies manufactured a car identical to the popular Toyota Corolla and marketed it in the U.S. as the Chevrolet Nova. It was a good car—lean, efficient, reliable—produced by American workers in an American plant. But GM embraced neither the Nova nor the management philosophy from which it sprang. Even as other Japanese companies—Nissan, Suburu, Mitsubishi—began setting up shop in the U.S. and employing American workers effectively, GM was reluctant to acknowledge its own managerial and organizational flaws. Instead, GM executives mistakenly pointed to technology as the answer to their problems. Chief executive officer Roger Smith fell in love with the concept of automation and spent $42 billion on new factories and equipment in the first half of the decade. Before long, the company was spending more than it was making. Worse, the technology failed to produce the desired results. GM's million-dollar robots made more mistakes than its human workers, and the company continued to produce the shoddiest cars in Detroit. One of the most infamous of GM's lemons was the Pontiac Fiero, a tiny plastic sports car that looked

great but had an unfortunate tendency to burst into flames. GM struggled with the Fiero's problems for several years, but never did get it right. In 1989 the company built more than 240,000 four-cylinder Fieros; each one was recalled...*twice*.

In late 1986, as Chrysler and Ford were surging, GM was staggering. A steep increase in the value of the yen had driven up the price of Japanese products in the U.S., and domestic auto manufacturers were among the first to benefit. The Japanese, however, fought back, first by expanding their American operations, and later by adding a line of popular luxury cars, most notably Acura (Honda) and Lexus (Toyota). Meanwhile, instead of exploiting their currency advantage by offering great deals, the Big Three got greedy and *raised* prices. GM, the company that could least afford this tactic, was stung most severely. When given the option of buying a Pontiac or paying $300 more for a Honda, the consumer invariably chose the Honda.

In 1991, GM's Saturn division emerged with a progressive look and marketing—and to quick acceptance from consumers. 1991 Saturn SL2 (opposite) and 1991 Saturn SC (above).

By the end of 1986 GM's market share had fallen to 34 percent. The company spent billions of dollars on its new GM-10 cars (which included the Pontiac Grand Prix, Chevrolet Lumina, and Buick Regal), introduced in 1987 and 1988, but public response was tepid. Mechanical problems plagued the cars. Sales lagged. Inevitably, GM began slashing its work force and closing factories in an effort to stop the bleeding. This process would take several years. In February, 1992, GM announced that it had lost $4.45 billion in the previous year; another 21 factories would have to be closed, thousands of jobs lost.

GM was the last of the Big Three automakers to take responsibility for its problems. Once galvanized, though, the company began to show improvement. Its unique and independent Saturn division—which enthusiastically adopted the Japanese team approach to making cars at its Tennessee plant, as well as a customer-friendly approach to selling them—won critical acclaim with consumers. GM also strengthened its European division (Opel in particular) and entered into an agreement with Toyota whereby GM would produce a line of its new J-cars for Japan. By early 1994 the transformation, under CEO Jack Smith, was nearly complete: a leaner, more progressive General Motors reported an annual profit for the first time since 1989.

General Motors' decline was the longest and most precipitous of the Big Three, and its revival the slowest to take shape; however, both Chrysler and Ford experienced their own problems as the Eighties gave way to the Nineties. At Chrysler, the trouble began soon after the stock market crash of October, 1987. Like General Motors, Chrysler had strayed from the business of making cars. Diversification was to be the key to greater profits and greater success. Instead, just like GM, Chrysler began losing money, closing down factories, and eliminating jobs. Before long, the company was in deep trouble once again; in 1989 it reported losses of more than $600 million in the fourth quarter alone.

Desperate times obviously called for desperate measures, and Iacocca responded accordingly. First, a planned merger with the Italian auto manufacturer Fiat fell through in 1990. Then, in 1991, Iacocca tried for the second time in a decade to sell Chrysler to Ford. And, for the second time, the answer was no. Chrysler went on to lose $795 million in 1991, and as the company's stock fell, so too did Lee Iacocca's. In late 1992, as Chrysler wallowed in fifth place in U.S. sales (behind Ford, GM, Toyota, and Honda), he was

eased out of the CEO's office and replaced by Bob Eaton.

By the time Eaton assumed control, Chrysler was already showing signs of recovery. Strong minivan and Jeep sales had sustained the company in rough times. Now a new line of "LH" cars—the Dodge Intrepid, Chrysler Concorde, and Eagle Vision—was garnering solid reviews. Introduced in late 1992, the LH cars, with their unique "cab forward" design, were sleek and stylish. And mechanically sound. The LH cars, created by a special team organized around principles learned from a detailed study of Honda, received glowing reviews. For example, William Jeanes of *Car and Driver* wrote that the LH cars proved "what we've known all along: if the U.S. automakers use their talent and resources, world-class products can result." One year later Chrysler unveiled the subcompact Neon under its Dodge marque. The Neon, with its peppy engine, smart design, and dual airbags, compared favorably with the best of the small Japanese cars and enhanced Chrysler's reputation as a leading proponent of automotive safety. Best of all, it cost several thousand dollars less than a Toyota Corolla. By the end of 1993, Chrysler stock was soaring again.

"The truth was, you used to see signs on computer work stations saying, 'Good, cheap, fast: pick any two,'" says Robert Lutz. "And my counter to that was, 'If Detroit is going to survive, we've got to learn to do good, cheap, *and* fast, all three at once. You can't say that you can get two but you can't get the third. That's a cop out, because many of our international competitors do indeed get all three. I think maybe the Neon is the first manifestation of Chrysler being able to do it good, cheap, and fast—all at the same time. The car is good, it's inexpensive, and it is very fast. And it's doing well in its segment."

Ford also stumbled during the recession of 1991, losing $3.2 billion. Thanks in no small measure to the revamped Mustang, though, Ford soon recovered. The original Mustang was one of the most successful and beloved cars ever produced in the United States. But it had lost much of its lus-

GM continued refining its muscle-car Camaro line with this 1995 Z-28.

ter over the years, thanks mainly to a series of ill-advised makeovers. The lean machine of the Sixties had grown clunky and unreliable in the Seventies and Eighties. The muscular little Mustang of the Nineties, however, changed all of that. Brought to market quickly, efficiently, and at a comparatively low cost, it redefined the way product development was conducted at Ford. And it was a hit. Popular with both motorists and the automotive press, the Mustang was named *Motor Trend* Car of the Year in 1994.

"The Mustang is a very strong brand," says Alexander Trotman. "It's a very important property of Ford Motor Company. The brand, I mean…Mustang. It's about a very exciting product, but it's also about value to the shareholder, as well as to the customer. So I thought it was good business to maintain the Mustang, and it's proving to be so."

The stunning recovery of the Big Three in the 1990s came at the expense of the Japanese. The Honda Accord had ruled as the best-selling car in the United States for three consecutive years, beginning in 1989, but in 1992 it was supplanted by the Ford Taurus. Interestingly, the Japanese, who had taught the U.S. automakers so much about management and production, fell victim to the same disease that had infested Detroit in the previous decade: complacency. The Japanese, like their American counterparts before them, had lost respect for the competition, and in so doing they had become overconfident and vulnerable. Making matters worse was an economy that strongly favored the U.S. The value of the yen continued to rise, driving the price of Japanese cars skyward. By 1995 the cycle was nearly complete: Honda and Toyota were closing factories and laying off workers, while Detroit was producing some of the finest cars in its history (the influential J.D. Power & Associates survey of quality placed four General Motors cars in its top 10 in May of 1995). Once again, the United States was the world's leading manufacturer of automobiles.

"You've got to understand that the American auto industry is an enormous success," says Jerry Flint, the veteran journalist who has covered the automobile industry for the *New York Times, Wall Street Journal,* and *Forbes.* "It has been to war and it has won. It is the dominant auto industry in the world. The Japanese came on strong and now they're back in Japan. That doesn't mean the Japanese are not going to sell a lot of cars here, but the American industry defeated their attempt to conquer the world."

The sleek design of the 1995 Mustang won numerous awards and became the vehicle by which many baby boomers revisited their youth.

CHAPTER 11

The Road Ahead

"In the past 25 years, it's been the period of the big wake-up call."

—*Robert Lutz, President, Chrysler Corporation*

There was a time when the U.S. automobile industry could afford to exist in a vacuum. Cars were designed, built, and sold primarily in America. There was no threat of competition, no concern with pollution, no complaints about overcrowded highways. The car was the great emancipator, Detroit its beloved creator.

Times have changed. Today the Big Three face a unique set of challenges. Survival in the next millennium is predicated on a willingness to adapt, for if the roller-coaster ride of the 1980s proved anything, it was this: Nothing can be taken for granted. Even as American companies learn to compete successfully with the Japanese, the environment in which the automobile industry operates continues to evolve. Gone is the

As the 21st century approaches, its promise will be complicated by issues such as overpopulation, pollution, and the need to sustain our quality of life. Adaptation will be a major task and opportunity for American industry. Research and development on alternative power sources for electric (left) or solar automobiles will become crucial if America is to lead developing countries—as well as itself—to a desirable future.

insular world once ruled by a handful of Midwestern executives. The auto industry, like all businesses, must exist within the framework of the new global marketplace.

It is a confusing, exciting time. No longer do the terms "American car" and "Japanese car" mean much of anything. Toyotas are being built in Kentucky, Nissans in Tennessee. Mercedes-Benz is planning to open a plant in Alabama. U.S. manufacturers, too, are taking their business abroad: Ford is making cars in Mexico, Chrysler in Canada. And the parts for these vehicles are supplied by distributors from all over the globe. Many countries now see what the U.S., Germany, and Japan saw some time ago: No other industry requires such a vast array of materials, processes, and technologies, or uses such large amounts of

capital, labor, and allied business. For this reason, countries once largely ambivalent about the auto industry—such as China, Mexico, Malaysia, Brazil, India, and Thailand—now see the car as a vehicle for their own economic development.

"I think today in Detroit you find a great deal of humility and an awareness of our own limitations," says Robert Lutz. "There is an awareness of our vulnerability, and an understanding of the need not only to please our final customers, but also to work very closely and cooperatively in an atmosphere of trust with the other partners with whom we must work, namely the union and the suppliers.

"When you talk about the industry going global, it simply defines what we've always known, which is that this is a worldwide competitive industry, and nowadays Detroit is competing with European firms and Japanese firms and Korean firms. Worldwide competition is now an accepted fact of life. Frankly, I think [globalization] is merely a new term for what we used to call

The creative design departments of the Big Three are generating exciting visions of the future (above), while the engineering departments will be responsible for maximizing economy, durability, and safety.

foreign competition. But I welcome it because it is a recognition of the fact that we no longer think we're the center of the automotive universe. We view ourselves as one player among many fighting for survival."

While the population of the world increased by 100 percent between 1960 and 1990, automobiles increased by *300 percent*. There are no indications of that trend reversing itself. In fact, as previously underdeveloped countries fully integrate the automobile into their societies, the numbers are expected to continue to grow dramatically. Many of these vehicles will be built in the United States; many more will not. In 1995, approximately 14 million cars and trucks were manufactured in the U.S. If that seems like an impressive figure, consider that it represents less than one-third of the 50 million automobiles produced worldwide.

The consumer, naturally, is the big winner in this equation. Never before has he been able to choose from such a wide assortment of high-quality cars. And it isn't just the American motorist who benefits from the spirit of competition. Just as the menu in this country was broadened by the influx of Japanese cars some 25 years ago, the Japanese buyer today has more options than ever before. Ford is selling approximately 50,000 cars annually in Japan, and it plans to quadruple that figure by the year 2000. And GM recently negotiated a deal to manufacture cars in China.

With automobile production spread around the globe, communication has become vital. The information superhighway connects designers, executives, engineers, manufacturers, and suppliers in such a way that product development—despite the distance between links—can actually be accelerated. Ford, for example, has seven design studios in various parts of the world, all connected electronically. The company can design a car in Dearborn and instantly send a three-dimensional image to a studio in England or Germany or Italy.

"In a way we're going back to the early days," says Alexander Trotman. "Now we have the tools, we have the communications, the computers, the jets, the faxes, and the interactive video techniques that give us the capability to design one vehicle that again can be made in various countries of the world, as was the Model T in the early 1900s."

The unfortunate fallout from globalization has been a drastic shrinking of the work force in the U.S. auto industry. Hundreds of thousands of jobs have been eliminated—permanently. Many of the workers who remain, however, acknowledge not only a genuine desire on the part of the Big Three to improve the quality of their products, but also a thawing of the traditionally icy relationship between labor and management.

"I think we're condemned to living with each other," says Robert Lutz. "It's a no-divorce marriage. Therefore, while we may not always share the same goals, and while we may not always agree with each other, I think both sides have decided that confrontation is potentially destructive for both sides. We can't get out of the relationship, so we may as well buckle down and make the most out of it."

At the same time, assembly-line employees note that they are working harder, faster, and longer. Through forced overtime, "outsourcing" (in particular, the farming-out of manufacturing jobs to Third World countries at a fraction of the U.S. cost), and automation, Detroit has been able to maintain production levels despite having cut its work force in half. A deep rift has thus been created within the UAW, where union members have been unable to agree on a course of action. Many workers believe the key to survival is to strengthen their partnership with management; others, including UAW Local 598 president Dave Yettaw, believe the relationship between labor and management is by definition adversarial and should be kept that way to protect jobs and avoid exploitation.

"I want to disengage from jointness because management has not joined us in our goals," says Yettaw, who started working at the Buick plant in

If you're going to function within a global community there has to be some machinery through which we can protect hard-fought and hard-won games. My father's generation struggled to win the eight-hour day and 40-hour week. It's down the drain now. And I think it will take another struggle to bring it back again.

And I am sick and tired of the corporate structure and their allies in the Congress, and the religious right that keep harping on family values when the corporate policy which has destroyed the eight-hour day and the 40-hour week has done more to damage the family life in this nation than any other single thing. And the trade union movement must assume its share of the responsibility for having remained silent and permitted that to happen.

In the United States, I think the auto industry is still backward in terms of committing itself to the kind of social policy that would protect workers' rights, consumers' rights, and the ecology of the nation. I think we are behind many other industrialized nations in the world in that kind of concern. I think we are behind our neighbors to the north in Canada, and if we want to influence the great nations and the people south of us through NAFTA or any other body, we better set a better example ourselves first.

Victor Reuther
Union Activist

"When you have an agreement on a person's workload and management comes by and says, 'Now, we've got to do this in the spirit of cooperation. We've got to do this in the spirit of partnership. We're going to add 15 more parts to your work area, and we want you five people to decide who is going to take the work. You're partners with us…but you can't decide to add any more people.' Well, that's a false partnership. And it is not our job as a union to help the corporation downsize to make billions of dollars in profit at the expense of eliminating our members all through the partnership and the jointness. I understand corporations have to make profits, but they don't have to

Flint, Michigan, 22 years ago, just four days after graduating from high school. "I mean…dignity. Is dignity saying what color you're going to get to paint the walls around your workplace? Is dignity putting in red, blue, and green lights rather than white? I think dignity comes with the pace of work. I think dignity comes with how management treats you. I believe dignity comes when they honor your seniority rights. When they live up to the agreement that says they will not subcontract your work.

make unheard-of profits. There's got to be something here for the community. We're all in this boat called Mother Earth together."

Speaking of Mother Earth…the automobile's impact on the environment continues to be a source of great concern and debate as we approach the 21st Century. Thanks to tougher emission standards and improved antipollution technology, the car of the 1990s spews far less poison into the atmosphere than the car of the 1960s; however, the sheer volume of traffic and the anticipated

The government has mandated that a certain number of electric vehicles (like the Ford Ecostar, above) be on sale by the end of this century. With the expected increases in their driving range between charges and top speed, they will eventually be competitive with gas-powered vehicles.

growth in automobile numbers make auto pollution an ongoing problem in modern society.

Automakers face mounting pressure to design cars that are not only cleaner, but also more fuel efficient. Nevertheless, most experts, including those at the Environmental Protection Agency, believe nothing short of a major breakthrough in automotive technology could significantly lower worldwide gas consumption in the next century.

Electricity has long been considered a possible, albeit flawed, solution. Battery-powered cars have less horsepower, a limited range—they typically require recharging after 100 miles of travel—and a comparatively steep price tag. Moreover, the mass production of electric cars presents an environmental challenge of its own. Batteries, after all, are

I don't think it's generally recognized that we've taken a huge amount of pollution out of the tailpipes over the last 10 or 15 years. Since the 1970s, we've doubled the fuel economy of the average passenger car in the United States, and we have taken about 96% of the tailpipe pollution out. By the time we get to the Clean Air Act requirements through the end of this decade, we're down to microscopic amounts of pollution coming from the tailpipes of new automobiles.

The big challenge is to get the old ones off the street. Some of the old vehicles are polluting perhaps 40 or 50 times more than a new state-of-the-art vehicle. So the really big issue is to change the fleet and get rid of the old ones.

Alex Trotman
CEO, Ford Motor Company

produced in power plants fueled by coal, oil, uranium, or natural gas. And when millions of old batteries begin to die, the industry is looking at a massive waste-disposal problem. Hydrogen also has been shown to be an effective source of fuel in electric cars, but it too raises ecological and economic concerns.

For now, it seems, the internal-combustion engine remains the most viable source of automotive power; and gasoline the most efficient fuel.

"We can make alternative-fuel cars; we do today," says Alexander Trotman. "We sell natural-gas vehicles, trucks, and cars. We sell vehicles that run on methanol and ethanol. We have a small fleet of electric vehicles on the street. But none of them can match the utility and economy and value for money of the gasoline-powered, high-volume vehicles that we know today."

For those who would seek to eliminate the internal-combustion engine, perhaps the most daunting obstacle is the affordability of gasoline. The oil crises of the 1970s are but a dim memory now; despite periodic price surges because of refinery problems or the onset of summer, there is generally no shortage of petroleum products, no great strain on the wallet when a motorist pulls up to the gas pump, and, therefore, no sense of urgency.

"Gasoline prices are so low that the Saudis are probably crying every time they go to bed," says Jerry Flint. "I paid $1.13 a gallon for regular the last time I went to the gasoline station. You know, in 1973 prices, that's like 45 cents a gallon. So prices have gone down since the great oil crisis. There is plenty of oil."

Although not solely the product of auto emissions, this Los Angeles skyline (April 1996) shows there is still the need for a great deal of improvement.

Sleek and sexy, these visions of the future actually serve to improve the engineering of a car, such as lowering its drag coefficient, which results in better gas mileage.

The auto industry and U.S. government have embarked on a joint program to design and manufacture a futuristic car that is safe, efficient, and environmentally friendly; a car capable of getting 80 miles to the gallon. Whether that goal is realistic remains to be seen. This much seems certain, though: As long as gasoline remains abundant and cheap, fuel economy will be a secondary issue with both car manufacturers and customers.

"As long as we have these low fuel prices, people are going to demand big six-cylinder engines, V-8 engines, even 10-cylinder engines, because fuel efficiency doesn't even make the radar screen on people's priority list," says Robert Lutz. "We in the industry advocate higher fuel prices—basically a 25-cent-a-year increase until we get to world levels—because we think it would set the framework that will convince people to buy smaller and lighter and more fuel-efficient vehicles. But without the stimulus of higher fuel prices, people aren't going to do it.

"It's not that people deliberately want to waste resources or don't care about the environment. I think they care about the environment very much; however, most people think that taking care of the environment is somebody else's responsibility, and that care for the environment shouldn't cramp their own lifestyle too much."

Consumers speak with their wallets, and what they are saying is this: *Give us bigger cars!* Indeed, not since the late 1950s has there been such a demand for size. The oxymoronic minivan has become the vehicle of choice for upwardly mobile suburban families, and the sport utility vehicle is one of the more ubiquitous status symbols of the Nineties. Both are big, expensive...and thirsty.

Granted, for a certain segment of society, these are practical vehicles. Particularly in the case of the sport utility vehicle, though one could argue that practicality rarely comes into play. The Ford Explorer, Jeep Cherokee, Chevrolet Suburban—all project a rugged, adventuresome image that speaks to the restless heart of the consumer, even if his idea of adventure is a trip to the local mall. What we drive says something about who we are; more important, it says something about who we would like to be and how we would like to be perceived.

"The off-road vehicle that is sold as a passenger car is a kind of wish-fulfillment machine," says Ron Edsforth. "We know because of surveys that fewer than five percent of the people who own these machines ever drive them off a road. Instead, I think, it's the fantasy of being in this powerful machine—particularly in this decade when we feel threatened by crime, by insecurity in the economy, by problems that are breaking families up. We want this sense of security that these huge, powerful, four-wheel-drive, truck-like cars offer us.

"You sort of get that feeling when you get in one, you have almost that vacuum-door kind of sensation: 'I've shut it all out. I'm now in control. I've overcome all of these problems and nobody can touch me. I'm safe here.' And that's a fulfilling feeling. It's far more powerful, I would argue, than 'Does this thing get good gas mileage? Am I emitting too much CO_2 into the atmosphere? To hell with it, if it is.' Really, that's how most people's minds work: 'This is the feeling I want in my car and I'm not going to think about these other things.'"

Eventually, of course, we will have to think of these other things. Gas is cheap and plentiful now, but with the automobile population mushrooming, many analysts still believe we could exhaust our oil reserves within the next 40 to 50 years. In

The automobile has diversified into several groups of vehicles offering various things to various people. While the minivan (such as the 1991 Ford Aerostar, above, top) is undeniably practical for family life and quite popular, the sport utility vehicle population is a more curious one. While analysts report that fewer than 5% of them are ever driven off-road, these brawny vehicles can deliver a psychological sense of empowerment many 1990's consumers seem to need. Shown here are a pair of 1995 Ford Explorers in their natural surroundings (opposite) and a 1995 Chevrolet Suburban (above, bottom).

Handling unlike any previous "Jeep," and with some indefinable je ne sais quoi, the Jeep Cherokee (above) has become enormously popular with a full spectrum of car buyers, including the luxury car market, and has spawned a plethora of imitators.

Jeep iconography is all about war, heroes. It came out of World War II, an idealistic war that men fought to get into. Jeep vehicles are about big shoulders, the cowboy's car, if you will; about freedom, this macho, inspired outdoor virility, it's a very American, American image.

Plus, the whole notion of feeling sporty. I mean, you don't have to be sporty. You don't drive them off the road, but the fact that you could, well, it's like when everybody started wearing sweatclothes. I mean, not because they were exercising but because it was chic to look like you did.

Women particularly love them because there is such a feeling of power sitting way up high and seeing the whole road and feeling in control. Nothing like it. I tell you it's a tremendous feeling to sit up high. It's marvelous. I mean, you feel like the king of the road. Tall, tall, tall.

And for a short woman like me it's fabulous. There are all sorts of advantages. In Greenwich, Connecticut, for example, you can look over the hedges and see the mansions.

Laurel Cutler
Automobile executive

I don't drive, never have. I've always been a streetcar buff. I like mass transit, especially if I can get a seat. Where I live now I take the bus. I still call it the streetcar. And it's near the beginning of the line so I always get a seat near the window and watch the faces. We do not have enough mass transit. It can be improved. If we had real mass transit, a good system, we'd have less cars, less pollution, less accidents, and less high blood pressure.

I ask how come the emphasis on cars, so little on mass transit? Well, it's a question of power, isn't it? General Motors, I think, has slightly more clout than I as a pedestrian have and that pretty much explains it. There's a bit more moolah there to pass around, is there not?

Studs Terkel
Writer

the automobile culture of the Nineties: clogged highways, air pollution, suburban sprawl, and, especially, urban decay.

An example of a modern city that has refused to surrender completely to the automobile is Portland, Oregon, which in the early 1980s became only the second municipality in the United States to exchange its federal highway dollars for a new mass transit system. A clean, efficient light rail system helped revitalize downtown Portland, while at the same time it slowed the growth of traffic in surrounding areas.

For every Portland, Oregon, though, there are dozens of cities where mass transportation efforts have failed miserably. That is why even the most ardent proponents of mass transit are quick to point out that theirs is but one piece of a very large and complex puzzle.

"You can't just drop a people-mover or a light rail car out of the sky and expect that it's going to give you urban vitality," says Earl Blumenauer, Oregon's state secretary of transportation. "You have to start with the basics, and that's commercial, retail, housing activities; streetscapes that people want to be on. Then mass transit works. But it's not going to create something from whole cloth."

According to James Kunstler, there is also a stigma attached to mass transit—in its current form—that precludes acceptance by the majority of Americans.

"If you look at our mass transit system, there's a very clear suggestion that it's for losers," Kunstler says. "You know, we might as well put a sign over the entrance to the bus that says, 'Losers enter here.' Because that's how bad it is, and that reflects our true attitude about public transporta-

the United States, simply stabilizing current gasoline usage would require a tripling of passenger car economy.

Car pooling, though, is a concept that has never really been embraced by American motorists, and it isn't likely to be in the near future. For the beleaguered commuter, the long, slow morning trip to work is often the most peaceful, private part of the day; the only time he feels as though he has any control over his life. There are no screaming kids, no barking dogs, no angry co-workers. There is only the sweet serenade of the stereo and the gentle hum of the air conditioner. Give up all that, just for the privilege of zipping along in the express lane—*the free lane*!—reserved for those who carpool? Not likely.

"The car is about pulling apart from the group and being the king of one's own universe, even if it's only two seats wide," says Laurel Cutler. "It may be small, but it's yours, and nobody shares it with you. It's being an only child again. It's being the first baby."

Mass transit has been vigorously touted as a solution to many of the problems associated with

Public transportation will be sorely needed to help alleviate the terrible traffic congestion suffered in many cities. Portland, Oregon has instituted a modern light-rail system which has been credited with decreasing the rate of traffic growth, as well as reinvigorating the downtown area.

*I*n the global economy, with cars being produced in any number of countries and sold as "American" or "Japanese," a new spirit of cooperation and progress has developed. While nationalism and domestic pride still rank high, a sense of synergism is emerging which will enable the industrial powers to produce truly revolutionary ideas and automobiles.

One of the most interesting features of American life is that gas is still cheap but people are finding it harder and harder to buy the hardware, the cars, to run the cheap gas in. You know, automobile ownership is becoming incredibly burdensome for the average American. It's estimated that it costs $6,000 a year for the average American to run his car. Now that $6,000 would translate into $60,000 worth of mortgage money, you know, and that's one of the reasons we have an affordable housing problem in this country, because people are taking all their income and putting it into transportation rather than into things like their homes.

James Kunstler
Historian

While heated debate continues regarding the future of the automobile, it is clear that the public is not ready to give up its personal "magic carpet." Advances in materials (such as lightweight alloy wheels, below) and design (right) are ensuring the adventure for the next generation.

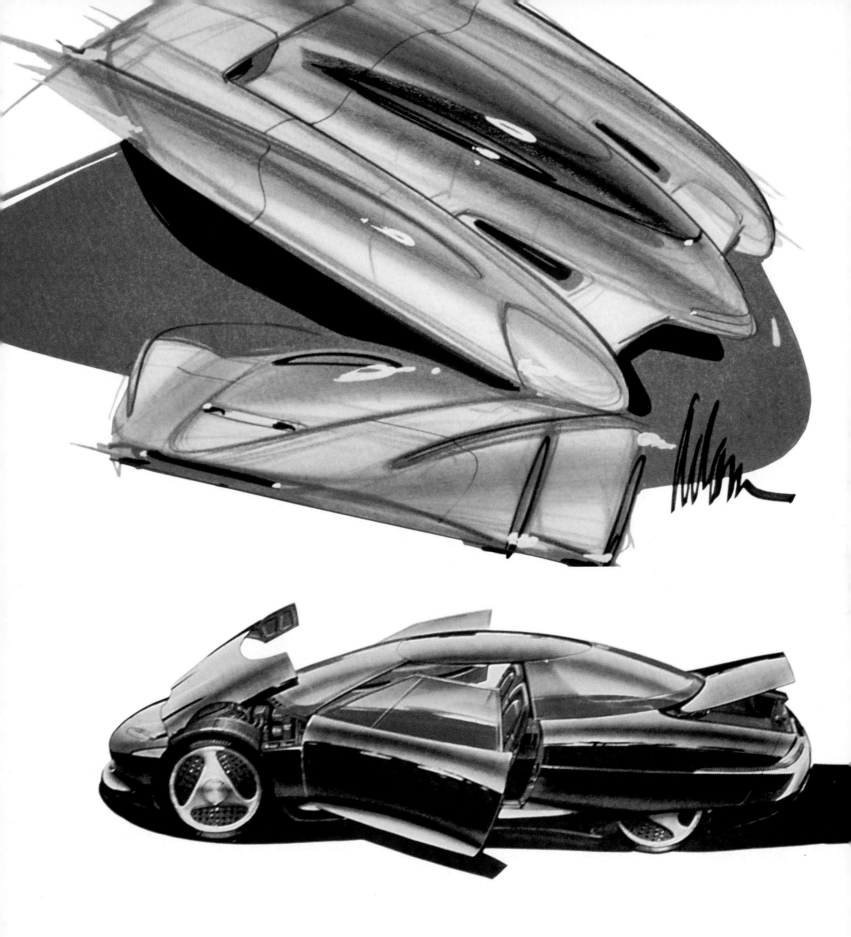

tion. We literally believe that if you don't own a car in this country there's got to be something wrong with you."

Even stranger is the notion of not knowing how to drive, as Studs Terkel has often been reminded.

"I was on a book tour once and I wanted to cash a check at my hotel," Terkel says. "The desk clerk said, 'I have to see your driver's license.' I said, 'Driver's license? I don't drive a car.' He said, 'I beg your pardon?' And suddenly he looked suspicious. So I said, 'But I do have a library card.' Then they knew I was un-American right there. A driver's license is your ID. That's your mark of identity."

At its very best, public transportation is a clean, safe alternative for those who happen to live along densely populated urban and suburban corridors. Realistically, though, mass transit represents a complete travel solution for such a small percentage of the world's population that it is almost ridiculous to suggest it will ever—*could* ever—replace the car.

In truth, the barriers are psychological as well as physical. Both in the United States and abroad, there is simply too strong an attachment to personal mobility for the car to become a secondary mode of transportation. Even in countries fortunate enough to have superb mass transit systems, such as Great Britain, France, and Japan, people continue to purchase and drive automobiles; in fact, in Western Europe the den-

Mass automobility is in many ways democratic. Cars are for everybody. The companies want to sell them to everybody We sell different cars for different people but we sell cars for everybody. In this sense, it is a force for a kind of integration. A sort of at least psychic integration of the country. We all become consumers, we all become car lovers.

This is one of the things that makes us Americans. And this is one of the things that people elsewhere in the world recognize as American.

Etoatin Shedlu
VP, Veblefetzer Inc.

sity of automobile ownership is approaching that of the United States.

"I think if we all are really honest, the form of transportation that we most like is our automobile, our personal automobile," says Dave Roper. "It has in it the safety. It has in it the control. I want to be in control of my transportation system, and what better way than putting me behind the wheel of my car? Now, can our society really afford that? That's the question."

It is a question most of us prefer not to ask, for it cuts to the very core of our passionate, often irrational, love affair with the automobile. It threatens a deep emotional bond that reflects who and what we are: dreamers, explorers, loners; a fiercely proud and individualistic people. Behind the wheel, on the open highway, we are more than the roles we play. We are transformed. The soft-spoken desk jockey shakes off the drudgery of another day and becomes a road warrior, his spirit lifted by the breeze at his back and the power beneath his feet. For most of us, that tug, that urge to flee…to fly…is irresistible.

So there will be cars. Today, tomorrow, 50 years from now. They may be dragged along at uniform speeds on computer-operated "smart highways." They may be fueled by hydrogen or batteries. They may be smaller, lighter, and yet infinitely more expensive.

But there will be cars. So long as there are drivers…there will be cars.

INDEX

Page numbers in *italics* refer to illustrations in the text.

A

advertising and advertisements, *28, 54, 56, 66, 68-69, 74, 75, 76-77, 78, 79,* 82-83, *94, 96, 98, 123,* 137, *138,* 139, 147, *230,* 231, *231, 241*
African Americans, 105, 107, 134, *134, 135*
air pollution, 232, *232,* 282-283, *284,* 284, 286, 290
American Bantam Car Company, 133
American Federation of Labor, *96*
American Locomobile Company, 72
American Motors Corporation, 147
antitrust violations, 171
architecture, roadside, 163
assembly lines, 38-39, 41, *50,* 51, *51,* 57, 238, 240, 246, 281-282
Association of Licensed Automobile Manufacturers, 38
Auburn Speedster, *114*
autocamping, 66
automobile industry, American. *See also* Japanese automakers
  executive lifestyle, 252
  federal regulation of, 225, 232, 234
  foreign plants, 280
  future of, 279-286, 290
  and globalization, 280-282
  Great Depression and, 88-89, 93-94, 95, 116
  Japanese automakers and, 242-243, 246, 270, 275
  mass production and, 36, 38-39, 41, *50,* 51, *51*
  in 1980s, 249-253, 258-259, 261, 270, 273-275
  in 1990s, 275-286, 289, 290
  "outsourcing" by, 281
  pioneers of, 11-62
  production of war materials by, 124, 126-129, *128-129, 130-131,* 131-134
  roads and highways and, 17, *19,* 20, 63-64, 66

troubles after postwar period, 226, 228, 231-232, 234-235, 238, 240, 242-243, 246
  turnover, 48, 51

B

Bennett, Harry, *96,* 96-99, 101, 105, 129
Benz, Karl, 13, 14
Big Three. *See* Chrysler Corporation; Ford Motor Company; General Motors
Breech, Ernest R., 143
Breer, Carl, 27
Buick, *123, 194-195*
Buick, David, 32, 56
Buick Century, *115*
Buick Le Sabre, *147*
Buick Motor Company, 32, *56*
Buick Roadmaster, *136-137*
Burton, Richard, *155*

C

Cadillac, 32, 54, *78,* 80, 86, 147, *158,* 182, *182-183, 191,* 198, *264-265*
  fins, 147, 148, 191
Cadillac Eldorado, *154, 228*
Caldwell, Philip, 228, 243, *247,* 249-250, 251, 252, 253, 254-255
California, 164, 166, 168, 169, *172,* 232
Chevrolet, Louis, *55, 56*
Chevrolet, 83
Chevrolet Bel Air, *150-151,* 186
Chevrolet Camaro, 222-223
Chevrolet Cavalier, 251
Chevrolet Corvair, 206-207, *207,* 209, 225
Chevrolet Corvette, *152,* 153, *210-211, 234, 266*
Chevrolet El Camino, *241*
Chevrolet Impala, *191, 217*
Chevrolet Mako Shark II, *212-213*
Chevrolet Nova, 273
Chevrolet Suburban, 286
Chevrolet Superior Roadster, *73*

PHOTO CREDITS

Detroit Public Library National Automotive History Collection: 10, 11, 12, 14, 15, 16, 18, 19, 21, 22-23, 25, 28, 30(b), 36, 38, 40, 42-43, 44-45, 48-49, 54, 55, 56, 58-59, 60(t), 60(b,r), 66(b), 67(t), 69, 70(b), 71(inset), 78, 80(l), 83, 92, 96(l), 100, 105, 108, 109(t), 109(b,l), 110, 112-113, 114(t), 115, 116(b), 124, 132, 135(l), 136, 138, 139, 140, 142(t), 143, 145, 146, 147, 152(t), 185, 186, 187, 188-189, 191, 200-201, 204-205, 207, 209, 210(t), 225, 253

Harrah's National Automobile Museum: 27, 30(t), 31, 33, 34-35, 46-47, 57, 68(b), 74-75, 96(r), 144, 148-149, 150(t,m), 151(b), 152(b), 190, 192-193, 194-195, 196-197, 198-199, 206, 208, 210-211, 212-213, 222-223, 224, 226-227, 228-229, 260

Road & Track: 123(b), 180-181, 234-235, 238-239, 240-241, 242, 244-245, 246-247, 248-249, 250-251, 254-255, 256-257, 258-259, 262-263, 264-265, 266-267, 271, 272-273, 275, 276-277, 278, 280, 283, 285, 286-287, 288-289, 292-293, 294-295

Peterson Automotive Museum (of the Natural History Museum of Los Angeles County): back cover, 2-3, 26, 60(b,l), 61, 62-63, 70(t), 71(t), 73, 81, 86, 87, 88, 89, 111, 114(b), 116(t), 117, 150(b), 151(t), 158-159, 182-183, 214-215, 216, 217(inset), 218-219

Collections of the Library of Congress: 8, 37, 64-65(b), 65(t), 76-77, 82, 85(center image), 90-91, 94, 95, 98, 118-119, 123, 131, 134, 135(r), 141(b), 160, 163, 164(b), 165, 166-167, 172

Archive Photos: 97, 103, 109(b,r), 130, 154-155, 156-157, 173, 202-203, 236-237

Dunbar's Gallery: endsheets, 4, 9, 53, 60(m), 66(t), 67(b), 80(r), 84, 93, 123, 160-161

AP/Wide World: 106, 174-175, 176-177, 178-179, 232
Bettmann Archive: cover, 120-121, 126-127, 128, 261, 291
FPG: 162, 168, 170-171, 297
National Archives: 141(t), 142(b), 164, 169
Ford Museum: 50, 51, 52
Movie Still Archive: 153, 189(t)
Photofest: 220-221
Volkswagon of America: 230-231
Deptartment of the Navy: 125
Chrysler: 1
Ford Motor Company: 233

BIBLIOGRAPHY

Bayley, Stephen. Harley Earl and the Dream Machine. New York: Alfred A. Knopf, 1983.

Collier, Peter, and David Horowitz. The Fords: An American Epic. New York: Summit Books, 1987.

Crabb, Richard. Birth of a Giant: The Men and Incidents That Gave America the Motorcar. Philadelphia: Chilton Book Co., 1969.

Flink, James J. America Adopts the Automobile, 1895-1910. Cambridge, Mass.: MIT Press, 1970.

Flink, James J. The Car Culture. Cambridge, Mass.: MIT Press, 1975.

Flink, James J. The Automobile Age. Cambridge, Mass.: MIT Press, 1988.

Halberstam, David. The Reckoning. New York: William Morrow, 1986.

Ingrassia, Paul, and Joseph B. White. Comeback: The Fall & Rise of the American Automobile Industry. New York: Simon & Schuster, 1994.

Jennings, Jan, editor. Roadside America: The Automobile in Design and Culture. Ames, Iowa: Iowa State University Press, 1990.

Keller, Maryann. Collision. New York: Currency Doubleday, 1993.

Keller, Maryann. Rude Awakening: The Rise, Fall and Struggle for Recovery of General Motors. New York: William Morrow, 1989.

Kunstler, James. The Geography of Nowhere: The Rise and Decline of America's Man-Made Landscape. New York: Simon & Schuster, 1993.

Latham, Caroline, and David Agresta. Dodge Dynasty. San Diego: Harcourt Brace Jovanovich, 1989.

Levin, Doron P. Behind the Wheel at Chrysler. New York: Harcourt Brace & Company, 1995.

Lewis, David L., and Laurence Goldstein, editors. The Automobile and American Culture. Ann Arbor, Mich.: University of Michigan Press, 1983.

Nader, Ralph, Unsafe at Any Speed. New York: Grossman, 1965.

Pettifer, Julian, and Nigel Turner. Automania. Boston: Little, Brown, 1984.

Rae, John B. The American Automobile: A Brief History. Chicago: University of Chicago Press, 1965.

Rae, John B. The American Automobile Industry. Boston: Twayne Publishers, 1984.

Sears, Stephen W. The American Heritage History of the Automobile in America. New York: American Heritage Publishing Co., 1977.

Smith, Philip Hillyer. Wheels Within Wheels. New York: Funk & Wagnalls, 1968.

Yates, Brock. The Decline and Fall of the American Auto Industry. New York: Empire Books, 1983.